Easter Readings to 1

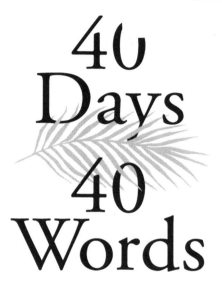

40 Days 40 Words

KEN PETERSEN
& RANDY PETERSEN

Our Daily Bread
Publishing™

40 Days. 40 Words. Easter Readings to Touch Your Heart
© 2023 by Ken Petersen and Randy Petersen

Requests for permission to quote from this book should be directed to: Permissions Department, Our Daily Bread Publishing, PO Box 3566, Grand Rapids, MI 49501, or contact us by email at permissionsdept@odb.org.

Bible permissions statements can be found on page 151.

Interior design by Jody Langley

ISBN: 978-1-913135-77-5

Library of Congress Cataloging-in-Publication Data Available

Printed in the United Kingdom
23 24 25 26 27 28 29 30 / 8 7 6 5 4 3 2 1

To Dad,
who gave us a love for words—
and God's Word.

Contents

Introduction

For us as brothers still in grade school, the celebration on Easter Sunday was an exciting event. We remember Easter mornings: putting on crisp new suits, walking into our local Baptist church "sanctuary" (actually a converted barn), and seeing an explosion of lilies and palm fronds decorating the platform in front. We fondly recall the congregation singing a particular hymn with its refrain, "Up from the grave he arose," which climbs the scale into a triumphant "hallelujah."

It was thrilling, even to us boys. We did not yet understand the full cosmic impact of Christ's resurrection, of course, but we knew that somehow, in rising from the grave, Jesus had saved us. This was the special excitement of this very different Sunday—exactly what Easter should be.

Later, as we learned in a Christian college more about the Bible and the early church, we became aware that there was more to Easter—that there was a Good Friday and something called Maundy Thursday and a day before that known as Ash Wednesday. And we learned about something called Lent.

We believed then, as we do now, that Christian faith needs to be real and not rote. We looked skeptically at certain church traditions, feeling that the faith we live should not be done simply because "it's always been done that way." Our decision to follow Jesus is personal and freely chosen, not prompted by the "ought to" of tradition.

And yet, along the way, we have made other discoveries about Easter. One is that Easter is not just a day but a whole season, an opportunity for special devotional time to bring us closer to Jesus. Another discovery is that some of those Lent traditions have solid roots in the Bible and are worth considering more deeply. And one more thing—many Bible people journeyed with Jesus in the days leading to His crucifixion and resurrection, and we might learn a thing or two by walking in those same shoes in preparation for Easter.

Looking back at our days in that Baptist barn, we reflect on that same hymn. "Christ Arose" starts with a somber grief, "Low in the grave he lay," echoing the agony of Christ's disciples and followers shaken by His crucifixion. Perhaps even as boys we sensed that the big celebration of "up from the grave he arose" was much more explosive because of the quiet opening despair of "low in the grave he lay."

And that's the point of this forty-day devotional book. Our personal faith in the resurrection of Jesus is made deeper and richer by engaging with the solemn journey leading up to it. The wilderness we sometimes find ourselves in is made more understandable when we experience the wilderness Jesus endured for forty days. The celebration of our salvation is more joyous when we remember the despair we were saved from.

This book is an invitation to walk with Jesus on the road to Easter.

Ken Petersen and Randy Petersen

1

Forty

*Jesus prepared for the Test by fasting forty days
and forty nights.*

MATTHEW 4:2 MSG

In the years following Jesus's life, death, and resurrection, it became the practice of the early Christian church to set apart the days leading up to Easter Sunday. This observance was officially adopted by the Council of Nicaea in AD 325 and became a period of forty days eventually known as Lent. But why forty?

Numbers seem to be important in the Bible. Seven pops up frequently and is considered the number of perfection, perhaps because of the seven days of creation. The number twelve is also common in Scripture—the twelve tribes of Israel, twelve disciples of Jesus, and twelve gates of the New Jerusalem.

Then there is the number forty, which appears all over Scripture:

The rain of Noah's flood lasted forty days and nights.
The Israelites wandered forty years in the wilderness.
The Israelite spies spent forty days scouting the land of
    Canaan.
Goliath challenged the Israelite army for forty days.
Jonah gave the city of Nineveh forty days' warning to
    repent.

Fasting, a practice associated with the yearly journey to Easter, is also biblically connected to a period of forty days: Moses fasted for forty days in preparation for receiving the law (Exodus 34:28). Elijah fasted forty days, leading to encounters with the Lord on Mount Horeb (1 Kings 19:8).

And there's one more "fasting forty" in the Bible: Jesus spent forty days in the desert fasting, in advance of His temptation by Satan (Matthew 4:1–3).

We might look more deeply into these fasting forties. We might think of them as *close encounters*.

For Moses, his forty days of fasting led to an encounter with God himself, the divine transmission of the Ten Commandments. Elijah's encounter came at a point where he was at the end of his rope and wished to die—but God came to him in the nick of time. Jesus's encounter was with the Evil One, Satan, who tempted Him three times.

We might think of the forty days leading up to Easter as our own personal close encounter. It is here we humbly prepare ourselves for what God has for us. Easter this year might come at a point where we need, like Moses, to rededicate ourselves to following God's standards. Perhaps Easter touches us when we, like Elijah, are at the end of our rope. Maybe it is through this season that we identify with Jesus in resisting the temptations of the Evil One.

That last point deserves more exploration. This forty-day practice of preparing for Easter ties Christ's temptation to His resurrection. But how are they connected?

We recall one of Satan's temptations of Jesus: "If you are the Son of God . . . throw yourself down" (Matthew 4:5). Satan adds that even if Jesus throws himself from the highest point of the temple, angels will rescue Him—no big deal. Of course, Satan's words are a trick: by throwing himself down, Jesus would be obeying Satan and not the will of the Father. It's important to put the temptation into cosmic context: Satan was luring Jesus at a point of human weakness to abandon His deity. In that, the fate of humankind lies in the balance.

Fast-forward to the crucifixion. Jesus is nailed to the cross. People passing by hurl insults at Him. They challenge Him, saying that if He truly is God, "Come down from the cross and save yourself!" (Mark 15:30). This sounds remarkably like Satan's temptation three years before, and it carries the same cosmic meaning: by saving himself, Jesus would have negated the salvation of us all. Again, the fate of humankind lies in the balance.

But we sometimes take for granted how hard it was for Jesus, as a human being, to endure the challenges put to Him as Christ, the Son of God. We know His death and resurrection were His destiny, but we overlook the possibility that it might not have happened had Jesus given in to temptation.

When in this Lenten season we identify with Jesus in resisting the temptations of the Evil One, it's not an obvious point or a casual thing to say. We should be soberly aware that it didn't have to turn out this way.

There's another meaning of forty in our preparation for Easter. Forty days of wilderness life and temptation are *hard*. While we might have good days, there are also bad days, and sometimes a lot of bad days. We live sometimes in a wilderness of work and home.

Jesus went without food, was tempted by Satan, battled the lures of the flesh, struggled with His closest friends who often didn't understand who He was, and endured ridicule and judgment from others. Some of that sounds remarkably like challenges we too face. Even though He was God, Jesus lived a life like ours.

Easter doesn't just pop up each year, happy and rose-colored. For Jesus, it was hard-fought and hard-won. Likewise for us, the forty days before Easter are a reflection on the wilderness we're in and the temptations we face. By walking with Jesus toward Resurrection Sunday, we share with Him our own dry, hungry patches of life, our own temptations and battles with the flesh, our own experiences of being misunderstood and judged. Because of these forty days, the experience of Easter Sunday means so much more. By walking with Jesus toward the resurrection, we come closer to Him.

It is the ultimate close encounter.

Preparing Your Heart for Easter

Take note of where those significant biblical encounters took place: Moses climbed a mountain. Elijah crawled into a cave. Jesus walked into the wilderness.

How can this Easter season be the same for you, an escape for a period of time each day into your own mountaintop or cave or wilderness, apart from the roar of your life? How can you enter a quiet place where your life might be changed?

In your home, schedule, or daily rhythm, where is your getaway place, your place to encounter God in a special way?

Lord, help me give you time apart from
the rat race of my life.

2
Ashes

I am nothing but dust and ashes.
GENESIS 18:27

One morning each year, a few of my classmates would come to school with a smudge on their foreheads. I thought it odd, figuring someone had just forgotten to shower that day. But there were two or three others who bore a similar smudge, and I couldn't imagine a bunch of kids had formed a protest group against bathing. Looking more closely, I made out a shape. A cross.

I learned this was a practice in some churches on a particular day weeks before Easter, known as Ash Wednesday. This was outside of my church experience, and I was suspicious of it at first. But I was informed this was simply a symbol of the cross. Some people sport the sign of the cross on bumper stickers. Others "take the ashes" on their foreheads on Ash Wednesday. In both cases, a person is saying, "That Jesus, I'm with Him."

Still, it was a curious thing to me. It was much later that I learned ashes are much talked about in the Bible.

The Hebrew word for "ashes" (*'eper*) is similar to the word for "dust" (*'apar*). In the Bible, the two are often used together and sometimes interchangeably.

In Genesis 18:27 Abraham pleads for God to hold back from destroying Sodom because his nephew, Lot, lives there. He is humble before God, saying, "I am nothing but dust and ashes ['apar w 'eper]."

In Scripture, both dust and ashes are often the result of destruction. After a desert wind demolished his house, Job "sat among the ashes" (Job 2:8). We see the "sackcloth and ashes" ritual practiced by Jeremiah, Daniel, Mordecai, and others (Jeremiah 6:26; Daniel 9:3; Esther 4:1, 3). Because of the association with destruction, ashes became part of a ritual of mourning. In such times, people would wear a coarse fabric called sackcloth and sprinkle ashes on their heads. Sometimes they would tear their garments.

Ashes also signify repentance from sin. When Jonah declared to the people of Nineveh that God was going to destroy them for their wickedness, the whole nation responded with sackcloth and ashes in repentance (Jonah 3:5–7).

Our wearing of ashes symbolizes all of these things—our humble acceptance that we are nothing in ourselves, that we sit in the rubble of our lives, that we have sinned and made a mess of everything.

By receiving the ashes, we identify with Christ's death on the cross. By this symbol, we say to the world, "I'm with Him, that Jesus, the one I call Lord."

For most of us, bearing a smudge on the forehead or sporting a bumper sticker with the sign of the cross is no big deal.

We may be looked at funny by some, but so be it. Yet for many in the world, wearing the ashes—identifying publicly with Jesus Christ—is cause for imprisonment. For some, this simple act of wearing ashes would be a death sentence.

We might remember that night of Jesus's arrest: Peter, facing the threat of Roman authorities, fearfully saying, "I don't know him" (Luke 22:57). We tend to judge Peter for his denial, but if we're honest with ourselves, we might have done the same.

Wearing ashes is a public statement about our Lord. It's our identification with others for whom the mark of ashes may be far more costly than it is to us. In a way, it's our chance *not* to be like Peter—to say, "Yes, I *do* know that Jesus. I'm with Him."

Preparing Your Heart for Easter

On Ash Wednesday we wear ashes in the form of the cross and enter a time of mourning and waiting until the crucifixion of Jesus Christ.

This is a time to pause and take stock of your life. A time of sober honesty. A time to fess up before God. A time to admit the mess you've made. A time to acknowledge to Him, "I am nothing without you."

Traditionally, the ashes used on Ash Wednesday come from the palms from the previous year's Palm Sunday, which are burned, itself a symbol of hope and mourning intertwined.

3

Abstain

Do not deprive each other except perhaps by mutual consent and for a time, so that you may devote yourselves to prayer.

1 CORINTHIANS 7:5

"What are you giving up for Lent?"

Of course the jokey answer is, "Broccoli . . . I hate broccoli."

Giving up something for Lent is now a meme of popular culture. Regardless of what church we identify with, abstaining at Lent has become like a New Year's resolution, a kind of self-improvement technique. We give up eating cupcakes, for example, as an act of overcoming a bad habit. In abstaining from a vice, we improve ourselves.

But this understanding of abstaining at Lent has it all backward. In fact, as with many aspects of the Easter season, it's not about us. It's about Him. Jesus.

The Bible tells us that Jesus went into the wilderness and fasted. Fasting is a different Lenten practice which we'll explore, but it's related to this idea of abstaining. Jesus gave up food when He went into the wilderness: "Jesus was led by the Spirit into the wilderness to be tempted by the devil.

After fasting forty days and forty nights, he was hungry" (Matthew 4:1–2).

By giving up something on our journey to Easter, we identify with Jesus's own abstinence in the wilderness. We acknowledge that Jesus, while fully God, was also fully human with the same physical needs we have. We recall His words from the cross, "I am thirsty" (John 19:28), a poignant reminder that Jesus was not above the pangs and aches of human flesh. Also, in becoming human, Jesus abstained from His advantages as God and "made himself nothing" (Philippians 2:7).

We give up cupcakes. Laughable in comparison, and yet meaningful in its own way. Our abstinence is really not about the cupcake but about the temptation. The next time we see a box of fresh cupcakes with mounds of fluffy icing, we are tempted. Our temptation is nothing like what Jesus faced, and yet perhaps in that brief moment of telling ourselves no, we connect with our Lord in a meaningful way.

The idea of abstinence in Scripture isn't always about food and drink. First Corinthians 7:5 deals with relations within marriage: "Do not deprive each other except perhaps by mutual consent and for a time, so that you may devote yourselves to prayer."

The larger sense of this verse is that abstinence refocuses our lives so that for a time we can better attend to our relationship with God.

Giving up something from our daily busyness gives us

more time to be with God in presence and prayer. In our world of social media and Zoom meetings and text messaging, we are constantly distracted. It would be interesting if we abstained from some of that, instead texting our hearts to God.

Preparing Your Heart for Easter

Remember that giving up something for the Easter season is not about you. So maybe you might think of getting beyond broccoli and cupcakes.

Think seriously about abstaining during this journey to the cross as an act of identifying with Jesus in the hardships and temptations He faced.

Approach abstinence with an eye to increased face time with your Lord. Give up something that gives Him more room in your life. As Eugene Peterson writes, "With less of you there is more of God and his rule" (Matthew 5:3 MSG).

Lord, help me choose something of substance and meaning to abstain from in this time. Help it to remind me of how you became human and identify with me in my daily life.

We might also think of giving up something as giving *away* something. If we look around the house, how much of what we own is just clutter? What might be donated to someone who might actually need and use it?

4

Fasting

*Is not this the kind of fasting I have chosen:
to loose the chains of injustice and untie the
cords of the yoke, to set the oppressed free
and break every yoke? Is it not to share your
food with the hungry and to provide the poor
wanderer with shelter—when you see the
naked, to clothe them . . . ?*

ISAIAH 58:6–7

Fasting is a traditional Christian practice, but it's relevant to our lives today.

We might think of fasting in terms of appetites and satisfactions. In our daily lives we eat what we want, consume entertainment as we wish, and indulge the activities that pleasure us. We satisfy our appetites. Our lives become very much about feeding ourselves. Constantly.

Fasting is the practice of denying oneself. It flies against this culture of consumption we live in. By denying ourselves for a time—food, drink, things, pursuits, entertainment—we take a stand, speaking out that something else is more important. It's a radical statement to our world that we are not simply following the norms, that we are choosing to be different.

In a way, fasting is the true culture war.

The roots of fasting in the Bible go back to the Israelites' annual Day of Atonement observance. The high priest performed a set of animal sacrifices in the tabernacle (later the temple) as payment for the people's sins. "On this day atonement will be made for you, to cleanse you," say the instructions in Leviticus. "Then, before the Lord, you will be clean from all your sins" (16:30). What were the people supposed to do? Take the day off, and refrain from eating. "It is a day of sabbath rest, and you must deny yourselves" (v. 31).

Most scholars understand the phrase "deny yourselves" to involve fasting, and that has been the Jewish tradition for centuries. But the Hebrew word is very strong, often translated "afflict yourselves." While it does not suggest self-harm, it's clearly a humbling action. Perhaps the logic is something like this: *While the priest is performing a sacrifice on the altar on your behalf, you need to make some sacrifice of your own, denying yourself the pleasure of food for a day.*

As we think about fasting during these forty days—giving up something—we should consider something that isn't easy, something not so casual, something that really, well, *hurts*.

Isaiah adds another wrinkle or two to the idea of fasting: "Is not this the kind of fasting I have chosen. . . . Is it not to share your food with the hungry and to provide the poor wanderer with shelter—when you see the naked, to clothe

them, and not to turn away from your own flesh and blood?"
(Isaiah 58:6–7).

The context for God's comment here is in a previous verse:
"Yet on the day of your fasting, you do as you please and ex-
ploit all your workers" (v. 3). As God responded to the indig-
nant hunger strikers, He noted that they were mistreating the
people around them. Could they really expect God to honor
their religious acts when their lives were full of violence and
exploitation?

If our fasting is to make a difference in the world, as we
plead with God to right wrongs, we need to make sure we aren't
an agent of those wrongs ourselves.

Additionally, the passage suggests that fasting is not ultimately about us. In fasting we are to refocus ourselves away
from "I" and "me." In this, we are saying, "I can do without.
Perhaps someone else can have what I'm not having."

Preparing Your Heart for Easter

As you fast during this forty-day journey to the cross, in
a small way you experience the significant hunger that many
others live in year-round. How can you share your "food with
the hungry" and provide "the poor wanderer with shelter"
(Isaiah 58:7)? How can you spread the love of the living Lord
to the people around you?

5

Lament

*Listen to my words, LORD, consider my
lament. Hear my cry for help, my King
and my God, for to you I pray.*

PSALM 5:1–2

Lament is a lost art.

It's an *art* because we see it most often in the Bible in the poetry of the Psalms and prophets. In fact the Hebrew word for "lament" (*qinah*) comes from a word for singing or chanting (*qin*). In Scripture, people's laments were songs of grief or mourning.

This art has been *lost* because so often we prefer to look on the bright side. More than a century ago there was a teaching that swept through churches about "victorious living." Many people learned to hide their problems because, don't you know, there's "victory in Jesus." Even today there are strains of this teaching that promote success and well-being above the hard truth of our lives: "If you express your pain or disappointment, well, it shows a lack of faith." Better to pretend everything is fine.

Make no mistake: it's good to positively trust God to redeem our situations, but the Bible also invites us to mourn honestly when bad things are happening. The biblical pattern is to present those cries and complaints directly to God.

Lament, in a way, is the biblical art of singin' the blues to our Lord.

———

God can take it. In fact He welcomes it. The whole of the Bible is about God's desire for relationship with us and His openness to hearing our predicaments. "Listen to my words," David sings blues-style (Psalm 5:1).

There's an entire book of the Bible called Lamentations. Generally credited to Jeremiah, it shows the prophet wandering through a Jerusalem in ruins, crying out in painful lament. It echoes that iconic painting by Edvard Munch, *The Scream*, depicting in a raw, guttural way the despair of life.

Lament is brutal honesty about us and God. The book of Jeremiah is full of such honest lament, as the prophet responds to people who won't listen to his warnings to get right with God. They preferred good news (see Isaiah 30:10), but Jeremiah insisted that only in the practice of lament would they get back to God: "Your towns will lie in ruins without inhabitant. So put on sackcloth, lament and wail" (Jeremiah 4:7–8).

Many of the Psalms are considered laments. (Some scholars put this label on 67 of the 150 psalms.) And the psalmists didn't hold back, crying out about injustice in the world, physical pain, depression, threats from enemies, and the fact that sometimes God seems to be far away and not taking their calls.

———

A fascinating thing happens in many of those lament psalms: the tone changes by the end. After lengthy sections scolding God, the writers often decide that trusting God is their best option.

For instance, Psalm 42 (continued in Psalm 43) gives us a verse-and-refrain structure that pours out several devastating complaints but always comes back to rest in God's goodness:

> Why, my soul, are you downcast?
>   Why so disturbed within me?
> Put your hope in God,
>   for I will yet praise him,
>   my Savior and my God. (Psalm 42:11)

Various genres of music (notably the blues) use a form known as call-and-response. Here the lyrics of lament take the form of questions (the call), and the ending is like a response from God.

On the journey to Easter, we mourn, crying out our complaints, expressing how we have been so wronged it makes us want to scream. Here we might echo the words of one biblical lament, "My God, my God, why have you forsaken me?"—words of the psalmist that Jesus recited from the cross (Psalm 22:1).

But a funny thing happens at the complaint desk: our lament turns to repentance. David writes, "For I know my transgressions, and my sin is always before me" (Psalm 51:3).

Like David, we come to this place of recognizing we are part of the problem. We have sinned. We need redemption.

And it is then, in this dramatic turn of laments, that we are able to see the cross with new eyes. The complaints we harbor in our daily lives are often a result of our own sin. Our tears are wiped away when we finally acknowledge our failures to God. Through clearer eyes we see that the cross is the crossroads of all that's wrong in the world and everything that's right in God's forgiveness of our sin.

Preparing Your Heart for Easter

Lord God, I have a list of complaints: _____.
But I know it starts with me, and so I ask your
forgiveness for these various ways in which I've
sinned against you.

6
Prayer

Out of the depths I cry to you, LORD;
Lord, hear my voice.
PSALM 130:1-2

Eugene Peterson once wrote: "Action without prayer thins out into something merely exterior. A prayerless life can result in effective action and accomplish magnificent things, but if there is no developed interiority, the action never enters into the depth and intricacy of relationships."[1]

Lent is a season of spiritually minded actions—fasting, self-denial, giving to others, walking with Jesus. It only makes sense that our devotional practices are saturated with prayer. Without prayer, our preparations for Easter will become superficial and exterior.

We might do well to think of this special time as an extended, honest conversation with God over forty days.

Some parents teach their children about an "outside voice" and an "inside voice." As in, "Please don't use your outside voice when I'm two feet away from you, resting on the couch."

Likewise, we can pray in both an outside and an inside voice.

We see many examples in the Bible of prophets, judges, and kings using eloquent language to communicate with God on behalf of their people. These were shared public prayers, probably not chanted in unison but offered up sentence by sentence by the individuals in the room for the rest to hear.

There's a place for that. But our prayers during this Easter season may need to be more of the inside-voice variety. The Bible lets us eavesdrop on a number of personal conversations, people of faith speaking intimately with the God they trusted in. Hannah begged to bear a child—"praying in her heart, and her lips were moving but her voice was not heard" (1 Samuel 1:13). Told that he would soon die, King Hezekiah "turned his face to the wall and prayed to the LORD," pleading for an extension (Isaiah 38:2). Jesus himself often went off alone to pray (Mark 1:35; 6:46), and we see His passion and love so clearly expressed in His beautiful prayer to God the Father right before His crucifixion (John 17).

These examples show us people in the throes of despair or great longing, their prayers coming up from deep within them, whispers and groans and growls of confession and yearning.

When in our lives do we talk with God from this private interior of ourselves? If not during our walk toward Easter, when?

There are different ways to pray, of course.

One might be in conjunction with fasting or abstinence. Substitute prayer during those mealtimes you're skipping. Pray to God at those times when you long for that thing you're giving up. Transform your longing for a physical thing into a longing for God.

Another approach is to "pray the Bible." Find a passage of Scripture, read it once to yourself, then read it again, this time slowly, focusing on each verse. A third time, read each verse aloud, letting the words blend into your own prayer to God. Pray the passage according to what it means specifically to you. Then read the passage once more, this time pausing to listen— listen for how God speaks to you through this Scripture in this very private moment.

Another way to pray is to use the form of the Lord's Prayer: "Our Father in heaven . . ." (see Matthew 6:9–13). It's remarkable for its simplicity, yet you can mull over it for a lifetime. The Lord's Prayer isn't the only prayer for you to follow, but it's a great starting point for the Lenten season.

If Lent is a journey with Jesus, prayers are the shoes you walk in.

Preparing Your Heart for Easter

Make this a season saturated with prayer. Sing the song, "And he walks with me, and he talks with me . . ." Make your song an ongoing prayer to Him.

Walk with me today, Lord. Hear my voice and help me listen to yours.

7
Repent

I take no pleasure in the death of the wicked, but rather that they turn from their ways and live.

EZEKIEL 33:11

In a common cartoon image, a long-haired, long-bearded man stands on a busy street corner with a sign that says, "Repent! The end is near!"

Whatever the punch line, there's a sobering truth in that image. People rush on with their lives, ignoring the prophet who warns them of impending disaster. They urgently need to stop, take stock, and change their ways before it's too late. But they have appointments to keep: "Sorry, I have a lunch . . ."

Repentance is a major theme of the Bible and echoes through the forty days leading up to Easter. Stop, take stock, change your ways. All of that is wrapped up in the word *repent*—and must not be dismissed because of lunch meetings.

Many of the Old Testament prophets called for repentance. "Say to them, 'As surely as I live, declares the Sovereign Lord, I take no pleasure in the death of the wicked, but rather that they turn from their ways and live. Turn! Turn from your evil ways!'" (Ezekiel 33:11).

The Hebrew word for "repent" (*shuv*) can also mean "return." The image used again and again is this: God's people have turned away from God and are going the wrong way. They need to turn back, return, repent. "Return, Israel, to the LORD your God," Hosea cries. "Your sins have been your downfall!" (Hosea 14:1).

The New Testament continues this tradition with John the Baptist—who probably looked a lot like that cartoon street prophet—preaching, "Repent, for the kingdom of heaven has come near" (Matthew 3:2). He baptized people in the Jordan River as a sign of their repentance. Jesus continued the same tradition, with the same message, as He began His public ministry (4:17).

This also became the call to action preached by the early apostles. In his Pentecost address after Jesus's followers received the Holy Spirit, Peter told the Jewish people, "Repent and be baptized, every one of you, in the name of Jesus Christ for the forgiveness of your sins. And you will receive the gift of the Holy Spirit" (Acts 2:38).

The Greek word used most often for "repentance" in the New Testament is *metanoia*. Literally it means a change (*meta*) of mind (*nous*). The Greeks loved the thinking process, and thus they often emphasized the mental aspects of life. But whenever we see repentance in the New Testament, it also carries the Hebrew sense of a turning, a changing, not just a new way of thinking but a new way of living.

For us who are saved, it's a little too easy to parrot the all-too-common words "Jesus died for our sins" and miss the point. The apostle Paul says, "[Jesus] gave himself for our sins to rescue us" (Galatians 1:4). Jesus gave himself up. It was either Him or us in the grand scheme of things. Jesus stepped forward and in some way that we cannot imagine took on himself our own sins.

In that light, what does it say if we come to the cross without true repentance? How can we observe the real meaning of Easter if we continue to harbor secret sin? How can our failure to repent—to change our minds and hearts—be anything other than disrespect for our Lord Jesus?

Preparing Your Heart for Easter

Has it been quite a while since you repented of sin? This Easter season is a time for you to do so. Consider repentance in terms of godly sorrow: not just your mental acknowledgment of your sin, but your deepest heart feelings about the cost of your sin to others and to God.

Father, forgive me. I have sinned and continue to sin repeatedly. This is a time for me to change my ways, to come to you to ask for a new mind and heart. Help me to be the person you've made me to be.

8
Heart

"Love the Lord your God with all your heart and with all your soul and with all your mind." This is the first and greatest commandment.

MATTHEW 22:37-38

A ruthless politician was rushed to the hospital with a heart attack. "That's a shocker," said a late-night comedian. "Who knew that he even had a heart?"

The joke works because the English word *heart* refers to both the physical organ in our chests and our emotional center. The same is true in the biblical languages. The Hebrew *leb* and the Greek *kardia* are understood physically and emotionally and encompass the whole of who we are—the moral and spiritual core of what it means to be human.

These words are used about one thousand times in the Bible. Most occurrences describe human motives, desire, decisions, or character. The *all* of us.

Your heart is who you really are.

The heart is notorious for bearing mixed motives, public pretense, and personal pride.

"The heart is deceitful above all things and beyond cure," the prophet Jeremiah complained. "Who can understand it?" (Jeremiah 17:9). The Lord led Samuel to reject David's brawnier brothers for the kingship because of their hearts: "People look at the outward appearance, but the LORD looks at the heart" (1 Samuel 16:7).

The prophet Joel challenged those who were making a show of their repentance, "Rend your heart and not your garments" (Joel 2:13). Through Isaiah, the Lord chastised some other phony worshippers: "These people come near to me with their mouth and honor me with their lips, but their hearts are far from me" (Isaiah 29:13).

At various points in their history the Israelites hardened their hearts toward God. One prophet called those hearts "hard as flint" (Zechariah 7:12). Daniel described the downfall of a Babylonian king: "But when his heart became arrogant and hardened with pride, he was deposed from his royal throne and stripped of his glory" (Daniel 5:20).

The heart is also the home of love.

Surely this is why the Great Commandment in the Jewish law is to "love the LORD your God with all your heart and with all your soul and with all your strength" (Deuteronomy 6:5; see Matthew 22:34–40).

As we walk with Jesus through the Easter season, we would do well to remember that God desires heart intimacy with us. Coming to a place of clarifying and purifying our heart is not dictated by the law but is an opportunity provided by grace. It's not a "have to" but a "want to." God loves us and wants to walk with us in close, loving communion. Why would we not want to have that?

As we journey to the cross, this is a good time to review our heart health.

Maybe we have wandered from God. The Bible advises: "Let us examine our ways and test them, and let us return to the Lord" (Lamentations 3:40).

Perhaps we harbor spiritual pride: "Do not think of yourself more highly than you ought" (Romans 12:3).

We might consider the words of Jesus as a model for what our heart health should be like. "Blessed are the pure in heart" (Matthew 5:8), He said, suggesting perhaps those who are honest in their intentions, not hiding mixed motives. "I, the Lord, search all hearts and examine secret motives" (Jeremiah 17:10 NLT).

God knows our heart. The question is, do we?

Preparing Your Heart for Easter

What is the condition of your heart today? This is a good time to consider the heart love of God and respond to it. This is a good time to pray for God to "give you a new heart and put a new spirit in you" (Ezekiel 36:26). This Easter season is a good time for you to come to God with more than just a mental agreement but a complete trust in the risen Jesus at the core of who you are.

9
Meditate

Blessed is the one . . . who meditates on
his law day and night.

PSALM 1:1–2

We normally think of devotional time, or a time of meditation, as a few minutes alone with God at the beginning of each day.

In a way, the Easter season is a constant meditation, one lasting forty days into Holy Week. It might still start for you with a morning practice of quiet time with God, but it is meant to be a continuing practice throughout the day.

Sounds daunting, but think of it this way: the journey to Easter is most meaningful when we are continuously focused on Jesus.

Meditation is something God commanded His people to do in the Bible: "Keep this Book of the Law always on your lips; meditate on it day and night, so that you may be careful to do everything written in it. Then you will be prosperous and successful" (Joshua 1:8).

That was part of God's charge to Joshua, the new leader of the Israelites after the death of Moses. Meditation on the law of the Lord also gets a mention in the first psalm. The "blessed" person finds "delight" in God's Word, and "meditates" on it "day and night" (vv. 1–2).

Sounds great, but many modern believers wonder what it means to meditate and how to do it.

The familiar passage in Psalm 1 speaks of meditating on God's law day and night. We already know that our "devotional time" involves reading the Bible, but we might pick up another shard of meaning from the paraphrased version in *The Message*: "You thrill to GOD's Word, you chew on Scripture day and night" (v. 2).

Meditation is not just reading the words of God but engaging with them deeply, with feeling and thrill, taking them in as if they truly are "our daily bread" (see Matthew 4:4).

The Hebrew word for "meditate" in this psalm, *hagah*, is also used for growling lions (Isaiah 31:4) and whimpering doves (Isaiah 38:14). This suggests that meditation on the Scriptures involved reading that was quiet but not silent.

People might voice the words to themselves and not to others. Some scholars think the guttural *g* sound in *hagah* makes the word an example of onomatopoeia—when a word sounds like what it means. (The English word roar can sound like a lion's roar, but repeating the word *hagah* deep in the throat can sound like a lion's growl.)

In our meditation time, we shouldn't be afraid to speak out

loud. And we might allow our responses to God and His truth to come from deep within, our inner groanings and praises finding sound in God's presence.

Thomas McKenzie writes: "As we look at Jesus, we're urged to confess the ways in which we nailed him to that tree. This isn't literal, of course. But if Christ is crucified for our sins, then it's our sin (those evils done and those good things left undone) that have, in part, placed him there. This is a powerful form of meditation, and one that is especially appropriate for this day."[2]

Another Hebrew word, *siyah*, also translated "meditate," seems to take a more mental (and less guttural) approach. The lengthy Psalm 119, in its 176 verses all about the Scriptures, uses forms of *siyah* eight times.

We also find it in the victory song of Deborah: "You who ride on white donkeys, sitting on your saddle blankets, and you who walk along the road, consider the voice of the singers at the watering places. They recite the victories of the LORD" (Judges 5:10–11). She is asking people to stop bustling about with their lives and consider (*siyah*) the great things the Lord has done.

Maybe that's the best guidance for us in our fast-paced lives. It doesn't matter whether we growl or moan or just ponder. But we might stop a minute. Slow down. Pay special attention to what God is doing.

Preparing Your Heart for Easter

During this season of Easter, consider other approaches to your devotional time. Start with stopping—freeing yourself from busy. Allow yourself to engage emotionally with the words of Scripture. Speak aloud your thoughts and responses. Allow your true feelings to come out, perhaps in growls or moans or simply whispers.

I come to you, Lord, with a soft voice and big ears.
Help me ponder your words for me.

10
Grief

Blessed are those who mourn, for they
will be comforted.

MATTHEW 5:4

Not too long ago, our dad fell seriously ill. His prognosis was dire, and we called in hospice. Hospice, of course, is a form of care that accepts the inevitability of death, relieving pain and providing comfort to the patient. For a week, our family observed Dad's long passing. We were grieving before he actually died.

The journey to Easter is like that. For forty days we grieve the death of Jesus before it actually happens on Good Friday. And we ponder our own spiritual death that made Christ's death necessary.

In the garden of Gethsemane, shortly before His arrest, Jesus told His disciples, "My soul is overwhelmed with sorrow to the point of death" (Matthew 26:38). The Greek word there is an intensive form of the common word for grief. You could translate this, "Sadness is surrounding me."

We don't know what Jesus felt in that moment, but we might surmise that His deep grief was not just about His impending death but also about what He was to die for. He likely felt the brokenness of the world surrounding Him, the suffocating clouds of sin that became the reason for what He eventually did on the cross.

So, our grief during the Easter season is not only about the death of Jesus but also about how we are culpable in it—His death was necessary because of our sin. In this, our grief becomes more profound and agonizing, and we cry out to God for forgiveness.

Some Christians feel ill at ease with grief. If they've lost a loved one, lost a relationship, or lost a dream, of course they feel sad about it, but then they feel bad about feeling sad. This just makes matters worse. And friends are quick to cheer them up, perhaps too quick, asserting that God wants us to rejoice all the time.

Scripture frequently observes a healthy cycle of grief and comfort. There is "a time to weep and a time to laugh, a time to mourn and a time to dance" (Ecclesiastes 3:4). As the psalmist says, "Weeping may stay for the night, but rejoicing comes in the morning" (Psalm 30:5).

Abraham mourned when Sarah died (Genesis 23:2). David wept over the fatal illness of his infant child (2 Samuel 12:21). And Jesus wept at the tomb of Lazarus (John 11:35)—even though He was about to bring him back to life!

Scripture presents grief as a normal part of life, and offers a promise to those who allow themselves to grieve: "Blessed are those who mourn," Jesus said, "for they will be comforted" (Matthew 5:4).

Grief is good. Necessary. We should not feel bad about feeling sad.

Christians at Easter rightly rejoice in Christ's resurrection, but many tend to skip over what comes before. Any therapist would tell us that while we should not dwell in grief, we also should not minimize it.

It's a beautiful irony that our inevitable spiritual death is reversed by Christ's inevitable death on Calvary.

During this "hospice time" of Easter, we would do well to grieve fully, to feel deeply these meanings of death in the ultimate story of God and us.

Our joy in the resurrection is richer when we truly experience the grief of everything that made the cross inevitable.

Preparing Your Heart for Easter

Father God, help me feel genuine sorrow. Help me grieve in the depths of my sin and for my part in the awful, yet glorious, outcome for Jesus on the cross.

11
Giving

Freely you have received; freely give.

MATTHEW 10:8

The Easter season is traditionally a time to focus on three pillars of Christian practice: fasting (doing without something), prayer (confession and self-reflection), and giving (donating something to others).

Of these, giving is the aspect of Lent that tends to be overlooked.

"For God so loved the world that he gave his one and only Son, that whoever believes in him shall not perish but have eternal life" (John 3:16).

It's probably the best-known Bible verse, it forms the core of the Good Friday story, and it uses a very common word in Greek, English, or any language. The verb "to give."

God gave His one and only Son over to the power of death so the people He loves could have the power of eternal life.

We see here a spiritual economy based on giving, and it's unlike anything else we know. God isn't selling us anything. He didn't rent Jesus out to the world. He doesn't hire us to do good deeds in exchange for a certain number of blessings. He gives.

"For the wages of sin is death, but the gift of God is eternal life in Christ Jesus our Lord" (Romans 6:23). The life we have in Jesus is a free gift.

And, in gratitude, we become givers too.

Indeed, Jesus talked much about giving.

He told a Samaritan woman about the living water He gives (John 4:14).

"I am the living bread that came down from heaven," He said on another occasion (6:51). And in case anyone missed the analogy, He added, "This bread is my flesh, which I will give for the life of the world."

He told His disciples, "Peace I leave with you; my peace I give you. I do not give to you as the world gives" (14:27).

And, getting back to the theme of John 3:16, giving was central to Jesus's mission. "For even the Son of Man did not come to be served, but to serve, and to give his life as a ransom for many" (Mark 10:45; see also 1 Timothy 2:6).

One recent trend in the practice of Lent is to connect the idea of *giving up* something with the idea of *giving away* something to others. Perhaps the bread you abstain from this season is literally bread you give away to those who are hungry.

Actually, this is more than just a good idea. It's what we're commanded to do as Christians. James exhorts us to "look after orphans and widows in their distress" (James 1:27). Sending a group of followers out to serve the community, Jesus said, "Freely you have received; freely give" (Matthew 10:8).

This is God's economy of love and provision. He wants us to incorporate it into our lives and make it our own.

Preparing Your Heart for Easter

Think of ways you can connect your own abstinence this Easter season with the act of giving to others. How can what you are giving up become what you are giving away?

"God loves a cheerful giver" (2 Corinthians 9:7). The context of this verse has more language about the blessings God gives us, but it's not transactional. The Greek word for "cheerful" here is *hilaron*, from which we get the word *hilarious*. While this passage is probably not describing a laugh-out-loud experience, there's a strong sense of delight as we give to others from the bounty God has bestowed on us.

12
Temptation

We have [a high priest] who has been
tempted in every way, just as we are—
yet he did not sin.

HEBREWS 4:15

When Bible translators encounter the Greek word for "temptation" (*peirasmos*, or its verb form *peirazo*), they can choose from several different English word meanings. Instead of "temptation," they might call it a "trial," or they might say someone is being "tested."

This word appears in John 6:5–6, where Jesus asks a disciple, "Where shall we buy bread for these people to eat?" Then the text adds, "He asked this only to test [*peirazo*] him, for he already had in mind what he was going to do." Jesus was not tempting Philip to go rob a bakery, but He was probably wondering if this disciple had a clue about Jesus's ability to feed thousands.

We see another meaning of this word in James 1:2: "Consider it pure joy . . . whenever you face trials of many kinds." That's our word for "temptation," *peirasmos*.

So the Greek word suggests in one context a test, like a multiple-choice quiz, and in another context a trial, a hardship we might have to endure.

Then scan down the page and see another use of the word

peirasmos: "Each person is tempted when they are dragged away by their own evil desire and enticed" (James 1:14). Here *peirasmos* carries a greater weight and is clearly about temptation to sin.

Lent is a season that specifically identifies with the temptation of Jesus in the wilderness. For forty days, we walk a spiritual journey as Jesus did, sometimes fasting as Jesus did, focusing on who we are in relation to God as Jesus did.

When the book of Matthew reports this event, it uses the word *peirasmos* in the sense of "testing," and many translations call this the "testing of Jesus." Yet that may be a bit of an understatement.

Yes, Satan begins his interrogation of Jesus as if it's simply a what-if problem: "If you are the Son of God, tell these stones to become bread" (Matthew 4:3). But the "pop quiz" gets progressively harder. "If you are the Son of God . . . throw yourself down," Satan says (v. 6). And the final question is the zinger: "All this I will give you . . . if you will bow down and worship me" (v. 9). At this point it would seem the "testing" becomes something more—temptation.

In His final hours in Gethsemane, before His crucifixion, Jesus took His "final exam." He prays to the Father, "If it is possible, may this cup be taken from me" (Matthew 26:39). Within these moments and words are wrapped a swirl of theological truths—Jesus's relationship with the Father, His purpose on earth, how His deity and humanity coexist. We do not know the fullest meaning of His prayer, yet we are left with a sense that Jesus could still fail the exam, tempted to avoid the human agony ahead and to opt out of the question He was on earth to answer.

If we approach this moment with the idea that the conclusion was inevitable, we miss the holy drama of it, the cosmic risk that was wagered. The life of Jesus, human being and divine Son, must have been full of temptation, with opportunities right and left to stumble and doom us all. It culminates here in the Gethsemane garden, and all creation holds its breath as Jesus provides His final answer: "Yet not as I will, but as you will" (v. 39).

In giving up something during these forty days, we stare temptation in the face. Our human longing may be a little thing compared to Jesus's temptations on earth, but it gives us a taste of them. In this, we identify with Jesus, who, though God himself, was also fully human like us—and we face the fullest meaning of *peirasmos*.

N. T. Wright observes that we might very well *expect* temptations as followers of Jesus: "The first Sunday of Lent, when traditionally we reflect on Jesus's temptations, is often a day for reflecting on our temptations as well. Anyone determining to make a fresh start, and to go forward with Jesus into the unknown, is almost bound to find that testing of one sort or another increases dramatically."[3]

So, we *will* be tested, but whatever temptation we face, we know that Jesus has gone there first. The book of Hebrews assures us that Jesus "has been tempted in every way, just as we are—yet he did not sin" (4:15). And also, "Because he himself suffered when he was tempted, he is able to help those who are being tempted" (2:18).

This is a time when we confront our struggles—and we are reassured that Jesus helps us through them.

Preparing Your Heart for Easter

Make a short list of the big temptations you face. What are those larger debates with Satan in your life? Review the account of Jesus's temptation in the desert, and note His responses to Satan. As you consider your big temptation areas, echo Jesus's responses in prayer as if they are yours.

> *Lord God, I ask that you might provide me the*
> *will to resist _____.*

13
Sin

*God made him who had no sin to be sin
for us, so that in him we might become
the righteousness of God.*

2 CORINTHIANS 5:21

Sin is what other people do.

That's a rather snarky definition, but it has some history. Jesus called out the religious leaders in His culture for having that attitude. They wrote off a whole section of society as "sinners" and criticized Jesus for making friends with them (Luke 5:30; 7:34). Meanwhile their own sins of pride, greed, and spiritual abuse were quite evident (Matthew 23).

During this season of Easter, let's correct that definition. Sin is what *we* have done. Lent is not a time to be looking around and pointing fingers. It is a time to be looking within and acknowledging how we have hurt others, ourselves, and God.

***

We might think of sin as a *force* and a *condition*. Before he committed the world's first murder, an angry Cain got a warning from God: "Sin is crouching at your door; it desires to have you, but you must rule over it" (Genesis 4:7). The *force* of sin in our lives must not be underestimated.

James might have been thinking of the Cain story when he wrote, "Each person is tempted when they are dragged away by their own evil desire and enticed. Then, after desire has conceived, it gives birth to sin; and sin, when it is full-grown, gives birth to death" (James 1:14–15). We find this pattern discussed elsewhere in the Bible: our *condition* of sinful desire leading to sinful actions, which result in a deadening of our relationship with God (Ephesians 2:1–3).

The point of examining ourselves as we journey to the cross is not some legalistic review of our errors: "These are God's laws, and I didn't color within the lines." The point isn't painstakingly following the rules for the sake of following the rules. God's desire is relationship with us. Sins are those things that separate us from Him, that deaden our relationship with Him.

The Bible makes it clear God wants us back. God is grieved by our sin, angered by it, and yet He consistently offers forgiveness. The prophet Micah gushes, "Who is a God like you, who pardons sin and forgives the transgression . . . ? You do not stay angry forever but delight to show mercy" (Micah 7:18).

As we enter into a sober and full acknowledgment of our sin, we might remember that word "delight." God wants to delight in us once again. God wants us back.

Preparing Your Heart for Easter

Make Easter a time when you come to an agreement with God about your sin. During this season, acknowledge how your sin has separated you from Him. Focus on Jesus who "'bore our sins' in his body on the cross, so that we might die to sins and live for righteousness" (1 Peter 2:24; see Isaiah 53:4–6). Ponder what Paul states poetically in 2 Corinthians 5:21—"God made him who had no sin to be sin for us, so that in him we might become the righteousness of God."

14
Clean

Lord, if you are willing,
you can make me clean.
MATTHEW 8:2

"Cleanliness is next to godliness."

The phrase is usually attributed to John Wesley, who used it in a sermon in the 1700s. However, he seems to reference it as a popular adage already in existence at the time.

Some believe philosopher Francis Bacon, some 150 years earlier, wrote about the idea expressed in the phrase—that there is a link between one's physical cleanliness and spiritual well-being.

The saying itself doesn't come from Scripture, but the Bible has a lot to say about cleanliness. And it's rather different from what we understand "cleanliness is next to godliness" to mean.

Throughout the early books of the Bible, being "clean" was immensely important and seemed to carry two purposes.

For the Israelites, rules of cleanliness were strictly defined for health reasons. Certain foods were declared unclean. Diseases would make you unclean, as would bodily discharges (like bleeding) or touching a dead body. Contact with items used in idol worship would also contaminate a person.

But cleanliness was also significant in the worship of God. "Who may stand in his holy place?" the psalmist asked. "The one who has clean hands and a pure heart" (Psalm 24:3–4). Unclean people were excluded from the tabernacle or temple. In some cases, they were exiled from the community. Purification could happen through a ritual washing or the blood of a sacrificial animal. Unclean objects might be purified with fire.

While the Old Testament strictures regarding cleanliness seem harsh to modern readers, some of them also seem . . . well, modern. Thousands of years before scientists understood germs, the ancient Hebrews were practicing quarantine, blood safety, and healthy food preparation.

Jesus upended the common understanding of cleanliness. Speaking to the Jewish leaders of the day, He said, "Now then, you Pharisees clean the outside of the cup and dish, but inside you are full of greed and wickedness" (Luke 11:39).

He was pointing out that religious people put on physical appearances of cleanliness yet spiritually were hopelessly dirty inside.

It is Jesus, of course, who provides true spiritual cleansing. As the book of Hebrews describes, "The blood of goats and bulls and the ashes of a heifer sprinkled on those who are ceremonially unclean sanctify them so that they are outwardly clean. How much more, then, will the blood of Christ, who through the eternal Spirit offered himself unblemished to God, cleanse our consciences from acts that lead to death, so that we may serve the living God!" (9:13–14).

Preparing Your Heart for Easter

This season of Easter brings us to recognize our impossible calling in the shadow of the cross. As often as we wash our hands, we are still unclean. Yet God wants us to pursue a clean life physically and spiritually. Our hope in this impossible pursuit is this: "If we walk in the light, as he is in the light, we have fellowship with one another, and the blood of Jesus, his Son, purifies us from all sin (1 John 1:7). Ask God to help you to live a clean life today.

Lord God, I sometimes despair of living a life acceptable to you. It seems that just as I take a step each day, I soon fall. Help me, Lord, to keep at it, to strive for a truly clean heart, despite my failures. I want to walk in your light.

Jesus spent a great deal of His earthly ministry healing people who suffered from leprosy. One "knelt before him and said, 'Lord, if you are willing, you can make me clean.' Jesus reached out his hand and touched the man. 'I am willing,' he said. 'Be clean!' Immediately he was cleansed of his leprosy" (Matthew 8:2–3).

Notice an important detail. Whereas the Old Testament law guarded against uncleanness being transmitted to a clean person, Jesus reached out and touched the unclean person, transmitting wholeness to him.

15
Confess

Come near to God and he will come near
to you. Wash your hands, you sinners, and
purify your hearts, you double-minded.

JAMES 4:8

There's a traditional prayer of contrition that starts, "O my God, I am heartily sorry for having offended thee." The story is told that a young boy goes to confess his sins. Remembering that prayer, he tries to recite it but gets a little confused about one important word: "Oh God, I am *hardly* sorry for having offended thee."

There may be as much truth in that story as humor. Whatever our church tradition, confession of sin sometimes becomes rote, and we ourselves may confess our sins in a manner more "hardly" than "heartily."

Easter reminds us to take confession seriously. In fact, a spirit of confession sets the tone for this whole season. As we journey to the cross, we recognize that Jesus suffered because of our sin. While we rejoice in the salvation He has achieved for us, we are painfully aware that it is our sin Christ had to die for.

This is a time for utter honesty about ourselves. It is our

own personal come-to-Jesus moment—literally. It's a time of genuine contrition, coming from deep within our brokenness.

Here there are no double-minded excuses, no pointing the finger at someone else, no "I did it because . . ." Here we approach God in utter shame for our sin. Here we throw ourselves on the mercy of God's court.

"If we confess our sins, he is faithful and just and will forgive us our sins and purify us from all unrighteousness" (1 John 1:9). The Bible often uses courtroom images to describe humanity's interactions with God, who can play the role of a prosecutor, a just but merciful judge, or (especially in the person of Jesus) a defense attorney.

The Greek word for "confess" is a legal term, just as it is in English. The Greek words for "same" and "speak" are mashed together to create a word meaning "to say the same thing" or "to agree." In court, a prosecutor says, "We believe you committed this crime. What say you?" If you confess, you're agreeing with the prosecutor that you're guilty.

Take a look at the surrounding verses in 1 John. This could be a script from *Law & Order*. You could stonewall (we're paraphrasing here), deny your crimes, say you haven't sinned, but you'd be lying. In fact, you'd be calling God a liar. Is that what you really want to do, pal? But if you confess, throwing yourself on the mercy of the court, the Judge is ready to forgive you.

And get this: your court-appointed attorney happens to be the Judge's Son. He hasn't lost a case yet!

There is another sense of the word *confess* in the Bible. Not only do we confess our sin, but we confess the truth about God. And we join with other believers to do so (thus "saying the same thing"). This is the sense of Romans 10:9—"If you declare with your mouth, 'Jesus is Lord,' and believe in your heart that God raised him from the dead, you will be saved."[4]

Confessing sin and confessing the saving work of God go hand in hand. When we acknowledge our sin, he is "faithful . . . and will forgive us our sin." He relieves our burden because Jesus took our sin upon himself at the cross.

Our response can only be one of gaping wonder at the awesomeness of God and what He has done for us.

Preparing Your Heart for Easter

Here's who I really am, God: _____.
No excuses. I confess: _____.
I acknowledge the truth of who you are and
wish you to be the Lord of my life. Take me
and mold me for your purposes.

16
Penance

*Share your food with the hungry, and give shelter to
the homeless. Give clothes to those who need them,
and do not hide from relatives who need your help.*

ISAIAH 58:7 NLT

The word *penance* only appears in two major English translations of the Bible. Rooted in the words *repentance* and *pen-
itence*, it began to be used in church contexts in the 1300s.
And that's where it's commonly heard today—in the Catholic
sacrament of confession as a deed a priest assigns for a person
to demonstrate their sorrow for sin. The Orthodox tradition
and several of the more liturgical Protestant groups also speak
of penance, though their practices differ.

But penance offers a useful understanding for us all. It
links two things: our deep regret over our sin and our public
acknowledgment of sin through helping others.

John the Baptist got at the heart of it. Like many revival
preachers to follow, he attracted many curiosity seekers. When
he saw some of the very judgmental religious leaders in a
crowd, he thundered, "Produce fruit in keeping with repentance" (Matthew 3:8).

No, he wasn't asking for grapes or figs to stock his food pantry ministry. He wanted people to act in a way that proved they were sorry for their sins and wanted to live better. He said, "Anyone who has two shirts should share with the one who has none, and anyone who has food should do the same" (Luke 3:11). So maybe the grapes and figs would be a good idea after all.

That's what penance is—a social expression of one's genuine regret for one's sin.

Isaiah addresses this as well: "You humble yourselves by going through the motions of penance, bowing your heads like reeds bending in the wind. You dress in burlap and cover yourselves with ashes. . . . Do you really think this will please the Lord?" (Isaiah 58:5 NLT). Our showy religious actions of confession are empty unless they cost us something real. "Is not this the kind of fasting I have chosen . . . ? Is it not to share your food with the hungry . . . ?" (vv. 6–7).

This is one of the great themes of Easter. Our self-denial of fasting and abstaining is not only a personal expression but should also be a social expression—not done for show but coming honestly from a heart that is deeply regretful for one's sin.

We sometimes hear of penance in a nonreligious psychological context that leads to a wrong understanding. When people feel guilty for something, they might perform some charitable act: "I know I messed up here, so I'm giving money to this organization over here." They assume that the good deed somehow "pays for" the sin.

This is not what penance is. Martin Luther sets it right: "For works do not drive out sin, but the driving out of sin produces good works."[5] As a sign of our sincere sin-sorrow, we offer an act of penance—"fruit in keeping with repentance"— not to earn God's forgiveness but in response to it.

Preparing Your Heart for Easter

The weeks leading up to Good Friday are a time to ponder your own sins that Jesus paid for with His suffering and death. Consider ways that you can express your regret and your commitment to Christ by helping others. Acts of penance don't earn you anything, but they show the true desire of your heart.

Lord, here's what I want to do to help someone else:
_____. I offer this without seeking attention,
knowing this itself is not my salvation. Let it be a
quiet symbol of my sin-sorrow.

One of the great literary examples of penance is found in Victor Hugo's classic novel *Les Misérables*. (You might know the movie or Broadway musical.) Jean Valjean, a poor man, is given lodging by a kind bishop, but in the middle of the night he tries to sneak off with the bishop's silver—and is caught. Stunningly, the bishop forgives him, and even gives him more silver, and urges him to use it for good purposes. Jean does exactly that, building a business that employs the needy and doing other charitable acts. This was his penance: not paying for his crime but showing his commitment to live for God.

17

Feasting

Therefore let us keep the feast, not with old leaven, neither with the leaven of malice and wickedness; but with the unleavened bread of sincerity and truth.

1 CORINTHIANS 5:8 KJV

If you're a good cook—or if you just like food—you might want to do a study of the New Testament counting how many meals, feasts, and banquets are mentioned. From Jesus's first miracle at a wedding feast (John 2:1–11) to John's vision of the future wedding feast of the Lamb (Revelation 19:9), significant moments occur with food around a table.

The key word there is *significant*. Feasts in ancient cultures were occasions of remembering and honoring and celebrating significant past events. But in our culture today, the idea of a feast has been lost, the act of eating often just a fast-food occurrence, alone and unshared.

In Bible times, the Israelites had a weekly feast in their homes, the Sabbath meal, with certain prayers and rituals observed as their day of rest began at sundown on Friday. It's likely that the early Christian worship service developed from this Sabbath feast. (Many Gentiles got their first glimpse of a Jewish Sabbath meal in the musical *Fiddler on the Roof*.)

Every spring, Jews celebrate Passover with a feast known as a seder. This meal is full of meaning, following a prescribed order commemorating the Israelites' passage from slavery into freedom (Exodus 12).

For Christians, the Last Supper, originally a Passover seder, is surely the most significant of feasts, when Jesus taught His disciples and prepared them for His death. That meal, of course, is reenacted by Christians around the world on any given Sunday in the act of Communion.

It is also where the observance of Lent comes in. Our walk with Jesus through these forty days leads us to the Last Supper. After a season of fasting and self-denial, we are invited into a feast. The moment is poignant: our joy of eating again is tempered by the sadness of what is to come.

We sit with Him and His disciples as He takes bread and says, "Take and eat; this is my body" (Matthew 26:26). A cup is passed around among us all. Jesus says, "Drink from it, all of you" (v. 27). We are aware that we are partaking of something immensely significant, something symbolic and mysterious, something deeply spiritual, enjoining us to Christ himself. Jesus says: "This is my blood of the covenant, which is poured out for many for the forgiveness of sins" (v. 28).

Preparing Your Heart for Easter

When you come to partake of Communion, think of fasting and feasting as part of a long history of God's work, significant events that lead you through Lent, into Holy Week, and ultimately to share in Jesus's death and resurrection.

Lord, thank you for including me in the feast
of Communion with you.

On several occasions, Jesus compared God's kingdom with a banquet or a feast (see Luke 14). And why not? We come together in joy, in bounty, to celebrate the Lord's great love. But Jesus specifically challenged the status systems that existed, and still exist, at such social occasions. Don't take the place of honor, He said. Instead, "take the lowest place, so that when your host comes, he will say to you, 'Friend, move up to a better place'" (v. 10). God's feast is a place of grace.

18
Flesh

*For the flesh desires what is contrary
to the Spirit, and the Spirit what is
contrary to the flesh.*

GALATIANS 5:17

Finding His three closest disciples dozing off while He prayed
in the garden of Gethsemane, Jesus urged them to "watch and
pray" to avoid temptation. "The spirit is willing, but the flesh
is weak" (Matthew 26:41).

Those well-known words might come to mind when you're
trying to give up sweets for Lent and your neighbor shows up
with a box of doughnuts. Is that what Jesus was talking about?

Sort of.

Used hundreds of times, the biblical words for "flesh" take
a fascinating journey through both Testaments, but they always
connect with physicality. The Hebrew word *basar* can refer to
animal meat, but it usually denotes the human body. As in
modern English, "flesh and blood" can indicate a family bond.

Often "flesh" stands for the whole human race. When
Isaiah describes how God will pave the way for His people to
return from their Babylonian captivity, he says, "All flesh shall

see it together" (Isaiah 40:5 ESV). Sometimes the emphasis is on human weakness, sometimes on the temporary quality of human existence. In a riff on God's mercy, the psalmist says, "He remembered that they were but flesh, a passing breeze that does not return" (Psalm 78:39).

In the New Testament, the Greek word *sarx* picks up the same theme. John's gospel announces that the Word of God, the eternal Logos, "became flesh and made his dwelling among us" (1:14)—Jesus, God incarnate.

But the apostle Paul gives the term a special meaning, employing it to describe a spiritual struggle we all face. "For the flesh desires what is contrary to the Spirit, and the Spirit what is contrary to the flesh. They are in conflict with each other, so that you are not to do whatever you want" (Galatians 5:17).

Paul's comments are easy to misunderstand. And this has everything to do with how we approach the Easter season.

We might think Paul is saying everything physical is bad, so we should deny our bodies and be completely spiritual beings. Not only is this impossible, but it goes against much that the Bible says elsewhere.

Reading carefully, we see that Paul is talking about control. What force controls what you do with your body? Will you let God's Spirit guide you, or will you follow your own physical cravings? Our bodies are not bad, but if we only feed our physical desires for food, pleasure, revenge, sex, escape, or whatever—without the control of the Spirit—it will spell disaster.

To avoid this misunderstanding, some modern versions translate *sarx* as "sinful desire." Or we might call it unchecked human desire and contrast it with God's Spirit guiding our physical actions.

We do well to remember that God himself became flesh in the person of Jesus Christ. God himself knows the struggles of being human. In fact, those physical struggles become our spiritual calling. As Oswald Chambers wrote: "The Christian life is one of spiritual courage and determination lived out in our flesh."[6]

By denying our flesh in a simple way during Easter, we confess to our God that we are so often driven by physical wants and pleasures. We promise in this one little thing that we are willing to deny our flesh for a higher focus, as Jesus himself submitted His desires to the Father's will when praying in the garden before His crucifixion.

Preparing Your Heart for Easter

Father God, I can count the ways my flesh, my physical desires, too easily take over my life. Give me control of those unchecked desires so I can focus more on you.

19
Self-Control

*For the Spirit God gave us does not
make us timid, but gives us power,
love and self-discipline.*

2 TIMOTHY 1:7

The Easter season is, as we've seen, a time to examine ourselves in the matters of sin, the flesh, and temptation. Much of this falls under the umbrella of a word that pops up frequently in Scripture—self-control.

The King James Version of the Bible translates the word as "temperance" or "moderation," which has acquired a Victorian sense and sensibility—the importance of being proper and restrained, coloring ourselves inside the lines.

If we delve more deeply into Scripture, we find a larger context for understanding what self-control more accurately means.

Greek philosophers loved to write about the qualities of a good person. So it's no surprise that there are several different Greek words for the quality we call self-control. Socrates, Plato, and later Stoic philosophers prized the ability to control human passions. Don't let your whims run your life, they would say.

They coined the word *enkrateia*—internal power. (The *krat* part lives on in words like *autocrat*, one who rules by oneself. A person with *enkrateia* rules his or her own inner life.)

This word is used in a couple of New Testament lists of virtues, including the fruit of the Spirit (Galatians 5:23; see also 2 Peter 1:6). It's interesting that Paul used the term in his defense before Roman governor Felix: "Paul talked about righteousness, self-control and the judgment to come" (Acts 24:25).

Sophron is another "self-control" word used by Greek philosophers and apostles alike. Here the emphasis is on a healthy, balanced, sane mind. Paul uses this word in describing our response to God's grace, which "teaches us to say 'No' to ungodliness and worldly passions, and to live self-controlled [*sophronos*], upright and godly lives in this present age" (Titus 2:12).

As you process this, put yourself in the mind of the Greek philosophers. They saw people driven mad by anger, lust, or pride. (A number of the great Greek myths tell these stories.) Because of these passions, people lost control of themselves. Or at least they lost their awareness of the world around them. So the philosophers urged their students to govern their own minds, to maintain a sane balance, to stay alert and sober. The best citizens of the city-states were self-controlled.

Now fast-forward to the New Testament writers. The Hebrew language didn't really have a word for self-control, but this culture knew a lot about wisdom. And the Jesus movement was discovering the wisdom and guidance of God's Spirit. So it seems the early Christians borrowed this powerful Greek concept of self-control as a key selling point of their faith: "You want to create good citizens with self-control? That's hard to do, but when we yield to God's Spirit, this quality grows within us, like fruit."

So, references to self-control in the New Testament were intended to emphasize to Greek and Roman cultures that Christians were responsible citizens of internal self-mastery and special wisdom.

The idea is not, as we sometimes make "self-control" to be, about becoming meek and nondescript, simply living within the accepted lines. Christians are to be distinctive and powerful citizens in our culture. That does not mean we must homogenize our personalities so we all act the same.

During this Easter time, this understanding may cast new light on those matters of sin and flesh and temptation. We do well to consider the verse: "For the Spirit God gave us does not make us timid, but gives us power, love and self-discipline [*sophronismou*]" (2 Timothy 1:7).

The Bible pictures our Christian life in terms of Jesus's walk to the cross, His crucifixion: "Those who belong to Christ Jesus have crucified the flesh with its passions and desires" (Galatians 5:24). Just as Christ died for us, we are called to "die to self," to put our personal desires aside and to become shining examples of Christ's life-altering power to the world.

Preparing Your Heart for Easter

Lord God, I know if I cannot master my own self, I will not have influence in my world. I confess I struggle with self-control in a particular area of my life. Help me, Lord, to come to grips with this.

20
Humility

*He has brought down rulers from their thrones
but has lifted up the humble.*

LUKE 1:52

Fun with words: instead of rushing to the Greek or Hebrew, let's consider English for a moment. There's a fascinating batch of English words that can teach us something important.

We *humans* were made from the soil of the earth, the *humus*. When we realize our identity comes from, well, dirt, it can't help but prompt in us *humility*. (And since we don't take ourselves too seriously, the whole situation is *humorous*.)

Those word derivations are humorous because they are true. God really did make us from dust (Genesis 2:7). Moreover, we are lost in sin, broken, and hopeless. If we ever had reason to think too highly of ourselves, the Easter season prompts us to take ourselves down a peg or two.

We might think of humility as a deep awareness that we are not self-sufficient. Thomas McKenzie writes, "The sense that I don't need anyone, that I'm fine just as I am under my own power, is pride. . . . If any person takes an honest look at themselves, they will see plenty of faults, imperfections, sins, and even evils. Humility is admitting this reality and recognizing that we need help."[7]

The practices of Lent are practices of humility: self-denial, confession of sin, abstinence, fasting. The wearing of ashes, already pregnant with meaning, echoes the humus we are made from.

Ironically, we learn the most about humility from the model of Jesus himself.

Look at Philippians 2:6–11, as Paul challenges readers to cultivate a humble attitude. He summarizes the story of Jesus, who didn't cling to His divine status but humbled himself to become human—and even further, to die a criminal's death on a cross. Because He humbled himself, God exalted Him, raising Him up to a position of eternal honor.

In His ministry, Jesus described himself as "gentle and humble in heart" (Matthew 11:29). Using His favorite term for himself (and a rather humble one at that), He said, "The Son of Man did not come to be served, but to serve, and to give his life as a ransom for many" (Mark 10:45). When it came time for His triumphal entry into Jerusalem, He rode not a warhorse but a donkey (see Zechariah 9:9).

Of all people who have walked the earth, Jesus had every reason to strut His value, His importance. He did the opposite. In His example, we might think about our own desire to seem important—and let go of it.

As we humble ourselves during this journey to Easter, we encounter one of Jesus's last acts on earth: as His disciples gathered for one of their final meals together, Jesus took a towel and a basin of water and washed their feet—the task of the lowest-ranking servant in a home. "Now that I, your Lord and Teacher, have washed your feet, you also should wash one another's feet" (John 13:14).

The ironies abound: the Savior of the world humbles himself to wash the feet of those who are made from dust. We who are humus-sinners are beloved by the one who was without sin. We who are unlovable are indeed His beloved (Jeremiah 31:3).

Frankly, it's humbling.

Preparing Your Heart for Easter

Perhaps the challenge of humility for you is not public boasting or presenting yourself pridefully. Perhaps it is simply a tendency to assert your self-sufficiency.

Think about the times this past week or month when you determined to go it alone, to forgo the help of others in a certain task, to convey the idea that you don't need anyone else. How might those choices be seen by others as prideful? Now think of how you do the same with God—trying to go it alone without His presence. Ask Him now to help you see these instances of self-sufficiency as a lack of humility. Pray for Him to work to change your heart in these things.

21
Holy

You must be holy because I am holy.
1 PETER 1:16 NLT

It should come as no surprise that the Holy Bible uses the word *holy* a lot. More than five hundred times. Makes sense: the Bible is the story of God, and God by definition is holy, the Holy One.

But when the apostle Peter calls us to be holy just like God, it becomes troubling. For us to be holy like God is hard to do. Actually impossible.

Even so, many people try, making this instruction something it wasn't intended to be. We pursue being holy through legalistic checklists, pious practices, and perfect church attendance. For some it becomes an obsession with trying to do everything "right."

In our preparation for Easter, we are confronted with this problem, which is in fact a profound truth and question—God is holy, we're not, so what are we to do about it?

"There is no one holy like the LORD," Hannah prayed (1 Samuel 2:2). Not that we need to be reminded, but God is different from us. Special, set apart, a cut above, off the charts.

On a holiness scale of one to ten, God is eleven.

We might recall the verse in Isaiah where God says, "My thoughts are nothing like your thoughts . . . and my ways are far beyond anything you could imagine" (55:8 NLT). This is God making clear how He is different, on a totally other level from us.

It's interesting that Scripture often uses images of God that depict His closeness to us. He is the Great Shepherd, and we are His sheep. He is the Vine and we are the branches. He is the Potter and we are the clay. These images emphasize God is like us. Indeed, Jesus is God in human form—precisely for the purpose of being "one of us" (see Matthew 1:23).

Theologians use two terms to describe these aspects of God. One term is *immanence*, how God is knowable by us as human beings, how we can connect to Him. The other term is *transcendence*, how God is apart and wholly other—how He is holy. As Tim Keller says, "God is transcendently unique."[8]

When Peter asserts that God is holy (1 Peter 1:16), he is reminding us that God is transcendent, set apart, just as in the Israelites' temple He was separated by a veil in a section known as the holy of holies.

We might prefer those loving, intimate images of God, how he is our Great Shepherd, for example. Yet it is His true holiness that is the basis for the whole story of God and us. We might wish that God didn't make such a big deal about our sin, but to do otherwise would make Him less than holy.

God is holy, we're not, yet we are called to be holy like Him.

We identify, no doubt, with Isaiah, who tells his account of being called by God. It starts with seraphim shouting out, "Holy, holy, holy is the LORD Almighty" (Isaiah 6:3). Isaiah becomes deeply aware of his own unholiness: "Woe to me! . . . I am ruined! For I am a man of unclean lips, and I live among a people of unclean lips, and my eyes have seen the King, the LORD Almighty" (v. 5).

Like Isaiah, deep down we *know*. We know we are unclean, sinful, messy souls. In the presence of a holy God, we become aware of our own failures and brokenness.

God is holy, and we're not. We're separated from Him. This is the problem.

Of course, the cross is the solution, right? Through Christ our sins are taken away, and we are made "as white as snow" (Isaiah 1:18). As the seraphim announced in the Isaiah account, "Your guilt is taken away and your sin atoned for" (6:7). Peter says, "Put all your hope in the gracious salvation that will come to you when Jesus Christ is revealed to the world" (1 Peter 1:13 NLT).

This is the Easter connection, how Jesus and the cross and the resurrection join us to a holy God.

Sometimes in our personal salvation stories we forget how the enormous divide between a holy God and our own troubled humanity was bridged by Jesus. Sometimes by jumping to

Easter morning we forget how the temple veil dividing us from the holy of holies was riven in two.

Perhaps it is in our preparation for Easter through this Lenten season that we live in the wonder of God's transcendence *and* immanence, marveling that we can in any way be special to the God of the universe yet cradled in the Great Shepherd's arms.

There is still the question of how we live *now*. Peter's admonition, "You must be holy because I am holy" (1 Peter 1:16 NLT), sits there, seeming to call us to impossible perfection.

It may be that we are simply meant to wrestle with this verse, returning to it in humility over and over, reminding us of how great our God is. It may be that in acknowledging God's transcendence we find greater assurance in His wisdom and His sovereignty over our circumstances.

And it may also be that Peter is calling us not to perfectionism but to be different as God is different, set apart from the world. Peter adds, "Don't slip back into your old ways of living to satisfy your own desires. You didn't know any better then. But now you must be holy in everything you do" (vv. 14–15 NLT).

Peter is telling us to pursue a life that pleases God, that walks with Him faithfully each day, that draws on His strength and wisdom through the trials and circumstances we face in life.

Preparing Your Heart for Easter

Holy God, help me to stand apart from the world and the culture of sin. Help me to draw from your strength in living my life. Help me to seek you in all aspects of my life.

22
Judgment

The whole world [is] held accountable to God.

ROMANS 3:19

All around us these days people are judging others. Social media thrives on constant shaming, talk shows slam those they disagree with, and even our neighbors are full of critical language. We live in a culture of judgment.

At the same time, the only Bible verse some people know is Matthew 7:1: "Do not judge, or you too will be judged."

It's absurd for people to try to fix others when they themselves need fixing. Jesus said it's like going to the ER with a fleck of sawdust in your eye, and the eye doctor shows up with a big plank in his or her own eye. (Sounds like a TikTok video waiting to happen.)

During this Easter season of self-reflection, let's get honest with ourselves about our own eye planks.

The first two chapters of Romans address this. Paul assumes his legalistic Jewish readers will applaud as he criticizes the idolatry and decadence of the non-Jewish world, but then he turns the tables. "You, therefore, have no excuse, you who pass judgment on someone else, for at whatever point you judge another, you are condemning yourself, because you who pass judgment do the same things" (Romans 2:1).

With this in mind, let's ask ourselves the same question: Do we live in the same hypocrisy?

The Old Testament is a soap opera of people turning away from God, being judged for their rebellion, and repenting . . . for a while. The psalmists and prophets bemoan the fact that wicked people get away with murder, but there is consolation in the thought that God will ultimately judge their misbehavior. Even the New Testament speaks of future judgment by God. Paul writes of "the day when God judges people's secrets through Jesus Christ" (Romans 2:16).

Judgment belongs to God.

Thankfully, the judgment of God is not the end of the story. If we continue in the book of Romans, we find it spelled out well: "But God demonstrates his own love for us in this: While we were still sinners, Christ died for us" (5:8). God's judgment on sin is countered by His gift of eternal life through Christ (v. 16). Jesus fulfilled the prophecy of Isaiah 53:5: "The punishment that brought us peace was on him."

That's what happened at the cross.

Bringing it full circle, it makes no sense for us to pass judgment on others when we realize that we are sinners too, deserving God's judgment on our sin, but spared by the loving sacrifice of Jesus.

Does that mean we don't care what's right or wrong? No! We want to please God more than ever, but we treat each other with a Jesus-like love rather than condemnation.

As Paul put it, "Let us stop passing judgment on one another. Instead, make up your mind not to put any stumbling block or obstacle in the way of a brother or sister" (Romans 14:13).

Preparing Your Heart for Easter

Today, try an experiment: In your every thought and interaction, stop when you find yourself being judgmental of others. In that moment, pray for God to remove your judgmental attitude and thank Him for saving you from the judgment you deserve.

Lord, I pray that you would stop me in my tracks when I start being judgmental of others. Remind me of your love and forgiveness, and help me reflect them to those with whom I struggle.

23

Baptism

Don't you know that all of us who were baptized into Christ Jesus were baptized into his death?

ROMANS 6:3

This season before Easter has a logical association with baptism. Jesus's forty days in the wilderness—the period that Lent emulates—began with Jesus's baptism in the Jordan River. And Easter Sunday is often celebrated with the observance of baptisms: "Various Protestant denominations also perform baptisms at Easter, seeing it as a meaningful time to express the new life of the convert."[9]

Of course, opinions differ as to the form and nature of baptism. This short devotion won't delve into those issues but may help us understand Easter a bit better.

The Greek verb *baptizo* and noun *baptismos* come from the simple word *bapto*, meaning "to dip." We hear that word at the Last Supper when Jesus mentions the betrayer dipping his hand in a bowl (Matthew 26:23; see Ruth 2:14 for a similar Septuagint use).

But of course forms of the word jump out at us early in all

four gospels with the story of John the Baptist. (You might call him the Big Dipper.) People flocked to the river to be baptized by him. And this was no seaside vacation. Clearly it had deep spiritual significance.

The Jews already had a washing ritual, the mikvah. They still do as part of a process of confession or conversion. The water represents the way God cleanses a person's soul in response to heartfelt repentance. And this is what John was preaching, urging people to repent of their sins.

John seemed shocked when Jesus stepped forward to be baptized (Matthew 3:14). It still seems shocking today. Why did the sinless Lamb of God need to go through a ritual of repentance? But when Jesus came out of the water, the Spirit alit upon Him in the form of a dove, and a voice from heaven indicated God's approval of Jesus.

We see, then, that in Scripture baptism carries the sense of washing, cleansing, and purifying. This is part of our walk with Jesus toward Holy Week, a desire to be cleansed and made new.

There's another biblical angle on baptism: two of His disciples, James and John, ask Jesus for a special place in His future kingdom (Mark 10:37). Jesus responds, saying they don't know what they're asking: "Can you drink the cup I drink or be baptized with the baptism I am baptized with?" (v. 38).

The language used here suggests that "the cup" refers to suffering, and baptism may symbolize death. In a way, Jesus is referring to a "baptism by fire," asking if James and John are willing to be overwhelmed by what Jesus will be going through.

Early Christians picked up this baptism theme when they faced the murderous opposition of the Roman Empire. They talked about martyrdom as a kind of baptism, and they went willingly to death in service to their beloved Lord.

As Paul explained it, "We were therefore buried with him through baptism into death in order that, just as Christ was raised from the dead through the glory of the Father, we too may live a new life" (Romans 6:4; see Colossians 2:12; 1 Peter 3:21).

This is, then, our challenge at Easter: Are we prepared to drink from the cup and be baptized with the baptism Jesus went through?

Preparing Your Heart for Easter

Lord Jesus, thank you for the new life that baptism represents, but also help me realize how baptism reflects the suffering you endured on my behalf.

The Greek version of the Old Testament, the Septuagint, also describes the leprous captain Naaman dipping himself into the Jordan River at Elisha's command using a form of the word *bapto* (2 Kings 5:14).

24
Deny

"Truly I tell you," Jesus answered, "today—yes, tonight—before the rooster crows twice you yourself will disown me three times."

MARK 14:30

Of all its layers and dimensions, Lent is probably most associated with this word *deny*. We deny ourselves some earthly pleasure to allow us to better focus on Jesus and the cross. We talk about denying ourselves Twinkies or Twitter in order to spend more time with our Lord.

But there's another aspect of the word *deny* that's a big bombshell in the midst of the Easter story. It's the account of Peter denying Jesus.

In mass-media terms, this event gets astonishing coverage. It's clickbait for sure, not only because Peter did what he did but because it was predicted by Jesus ahead of time. It has all the elements of a juicy story.

All the major networks—Matthew, Mark, Luke, John—carried it. They all reported both the prediction and the denial. And John, always seeking the bigger picture, tenderly recounts Peter's restoration—his later return to grace, an opportunity to profess his love for Jesus after His resurrection.

Considering that Peter was a major leader of the early church, it's remarkable that this story gets so much coverage. You'd think that church authorities would want to repress this story to protect Peter's reputation. But the story runs anyway. When you think about it, this helps to establish the truthfulness of the gospel accounts. If they were just making this up, wouldn't they have painted their fearless leader as more, well, fearless?

According to tradition, Peter was the major source for Mark's gospel, so kudos to him for sharing this shameful scene. Matthew and Luke cribbed off Mark's paper, but John was writing later with a unique purpose, exploring the character of Jesus. It's not surprising that John uses this story and adds a coda that reveals the forgiving nature of the Savior.

We often think of the word *deny* in connection with statements of fact or fiction. We deny that something is true. We say it never happened. The idea is false. (In this way, it's the opposite of *confess*, with its basic meaning of agreement.)

Peter's denial includes this sense of the word. Bystanders suggested he was a follower of Jesus, and he denied the truth of that statement. But the Greek word (*arneomai*) is not only used about ideas and concepts but also used with people. When you deny a *person*, not just an idea, you dispute any connection with that person. In modern terms, it's like removing a person from your contact list. This was how Jesus phrased it to Peter in predicting the event: "You yourself will disown me three times" (Mark 14:30).

This is the real weight of *arneomai*: Peter disowned Jesus.

Before we judge Peter too harshly, we might try to stand in his shoes.

This idea of denying or disowning the Lord became very important for the early church as it faced persecution. Denying Jesus might save your temporal, physical life, but it would put your eternal life in jeopardy.

Many of us live in places that allow a relative measure of freedom in professing Jesus. But some Christians live in cultures where mentioning the name of Jesus might cost them their lives. What would you do in such a situation?

Still, the lesson at hand is more than that. What if Peter's response was simply not answering at all? What if he had remained silent? Would that also have been a denial of Jesus? We can easily imagine Peter later hemming and hawing over the technicalities: "Now, look, I never *said* I didn't know him."

How often do we deny our faith in Jesus Christ by remaining silent?

It is John who provides a beautiful account of Peter's restoration. Jesus asks Peter, "Do you love me?" (John 21:15).

Peter says, "Yes, Lord . . . you know that I love you." And Jesus replies, "Feed my lambs."

This is generally regarded as Jesus expressing trust in Peter to care for the flock of believers Jesus would soon be leaving behind. It's a tender example of Jesus forgiving Peter for his earlier denial.

He forgives us too.

Preparing Your Heart for Easter

In this Easter season, consider your own profession of faith in Jesus. Is He a secret part of your life, or do others know that you follow Him?

25
Forgive

*And forgive us our debts, as we also
have forgiven our debtors.*

MATTHEW 6:12

It is perhaps the most shocking thing ever said: a man being crucified looks at His tormentors and prays, "Father, forgive them, for they do not know what they are doing" (Luke 23:34).

Most of us are familiar with the seven last words from the cross collected from the four gospels. We've heard so many sermons on these sayings that we could preach them ourselves. But don't let familiarity breed neglect. In His first utterance from the cross, Jesus said something astounding here, asking forgiveness for those who were in the act of killing Him.

It's all the more amazing when we recognize that His death was the way God would forgive them. Jesus was in the very act of dying for their sins. And ours.

In the New Testament, forgiveness moves both vertically and horizontally. That is, God forgives us, but we are also expected to forgive others. In the Lord's Prayer, the two are linked: "And forgive us our sins, for we ourselves forgive everyone who is indebted to us" (Luke 11:4 ESV).

Forgiveness starts with a deep awareness of our own sin. Keith Potter writes: "We are forever underestimating the seriousness of sin and its effects, making us unlike God and unfit for his good fellowship. Our efforts at forgiving ourselves and others will be thin and hollow as well unless we understand how God's grace so completely covers us through Jesus Christ, making us righteous in God's eyes and fit for his good fellowship."[10]

It's only when we deeply understand God's forgiveness of our sin that our forgiveness of others takes on real meaning and depth.

Peter once asked Jesus how many times he should forgive someone. Always the disciple bent on outdoing everyone else, Peter said, "Up to seven times?" (Matthew 18:21). Jesus trumped him, saying "seventy-seven"—essentially an infinite amount (v. 22). In other words, it's not how many times you forgive someone but the depth and expanse of your forgiveness. It's not a number, Peter. Forgiveness needs to be unlimited.

The Easter season is a time for forgiving others in light of how God has forgiven us through the cross. It's not a checkbox we tick off on our to-do list. It's a considered, prayerful, intentional reconciliation of accounts with those who have wronged us, even perhaps in grievous ways. After all, this is what Christ did for us.

As Paul wrote, "Bear with each other and forgive one another if any of you has a grievance against someone. Forgive as the Lord forgave you" (Colossians 3:13).

Preparing Your Heart for Easter

Lord God, there is one person in my life who has so deeply hurt me, it feels impossible for me to forgive. I know you have forgiven me for some terrible things. Help me extend that grace to this person who has wronged me.

26
Desert

*I thirst for you, my whole being longs
for you, in a dry and parched land
where there is no water.*

PSALM 63:1

Perhaps you've gone hiking or camping in a woodsy "wilderness." If so, you'd be forgiven for thinking that the Israelites wandered through a wilderness of leafy trees and babbling brooks. Not so. They journeyed through a desert. While there were pockets of habitable land—Moses had once tended sheep in the region—much of the terrain was dry and barren.

Sometimes we go through stretches of life that feel desolate. Everything is dreary sameness. We feel weathered by the troubles of life.

The Lenten season is an acknowledgment that we live in a desert sometimes. We may be familiar with S. M. Lockridge's catchy phrase "It's Friday, but Sunday's Coming!" Yes, but for us in this moment right now, it's still Good Friday.

Ronald Rolheiser writes: "Lent invites us to stop eating, so to speak, whatever protects us from having to face the desert that is inside of us. It invites us to feel our smallness, to feel our vulnerability, to feel our fears, and to open ourselves to the chaos of the desert so that we can finally give the angels a chance to feed us."[11]

We might do well to approach our wilderness differently. This is a time of testing, of reminding us of how desperately inadequate we are, of making us aware of our deep need for God.

Perhaps we need to embrace our inner desert.

***

One person we might take a lesson from: Moses. Len Woods writes: "Someone has observed that Moses spent his first forty years in the royal palace thinking he was somebody, his next forty years in the deserts of Midian realizing he was nobody, and his last forty years seeing what God Almighty can do through a nobody who obeys him."[12]

For Moses and the Israelites, the question was why. Why is our wilderness journey necessary?

The Bible explains: "Remember how the LORD your God led you all the way in the wilderness these forty years, to humble and test you. . . . Know then in your heart that as a man disciplines his son, so the LORD your God disciplines you" (Deuteronomy 8:2, 5).

It is only human to want to escape our present darkness, but we should be mindful that the desert we're in may be the work of God in our lives. Parched tongues make us thirsty for God.

***

Lent is a mini wilderness of forty days in which we experience a touch of the desert. Yet it points to an Easter of hope.

We are like those in the early days of the first century, tired and parched, dry as dust. We hear the booming voice of John the Baptist "preaching in the wilderness of Judea" (Matthew 3:1), calling for repentance and also announcing the imminent arrival of Jesus. It gives us the sound of hope.

As Scott Cairns says, "Even in the dryness of our desert journey, we are offered a sustaining taste of the sweet, the living waters. Even amid the gloom, we apprehend a glimmer of the light."[13]

We might then recall the words of Isaiah prophesying the coming of Christ: "I will turn the desert into pools of water, and the parched ground into springs" (Isaiah 41:18). This is just one of several Old Testament prophecies about the desert being transformed, made new.

God can transform your desert too.

Preparing Your Heart for Easter

Maybe the desert you're in comes with silence. Maybe in that silence you can better hear God calling you. Maybe you can hear His voice counseling you for His great purpose. What does this wilderness teach you?

Lord God, help me listen in the silence.

Old Testament Hebrew has two words for desert—*midbar* and *arabah*—but there is little distinction in meaning. *Arabah* is a common noun but also used as a proper name for the desolate rift that continues south of the Dead Sea—the Arabah. New Testament Greek uses the word *eremos* almost exclusively to describe desert wilderness. It carries the idea of "isolated place."

27
Conversion

You turned to God from idols to serve
the living and true God.
1 THESSALONIANS 1:9

We tend to think of conversion as a point in time when someone leaves a former religion, or perhaps atheism, and decides to become a Christian. In the case of the apostle Paul, this was a dramatic event on the Damascus Road. In the case of Chuck Colson, a lawyer involved in the Watergate scandal, it was a moment in a car at night when, moved by the Christian testimony of a friend, he cried out to Jesus.

We rightly thrill to conversion stories like these. But what if we thought of conversion in a different way, one that is not a single moment in time but a series of moments throughout our lives?

The English words *conversion* and *convert* come from a Latin root for "turning." An *advert*isement turns your attention toward something. When you r*evert*, you turn back. Di*vert* a stream to turn it away. The prefix *con-* generally has the sense of "with" or "together," so we might say *con*version is a turning in order to be together with someone, or perhaps some belief. If previously you were against, now you're to-gether with.

Conversion is often embodied in the phrase "turn to God." And it begs the question, "Turn to God from what?"

The answer occurs in the opening lines of Paul's first letter to the church at Thessalonica, on the Greek coast. People were talking about this church, he said. "They tell how you turned to God from idols to serve the living and true God" (1:9).

If we think of conversion this way, as a turning away from idols toward the true God, it prompts us to reflect on the idols we harbor in our own lives.

We might recall the folk-rock melody of one song in the musical *Godspell*, "Turn Back, O Man." The lyrics begin, "Turn back, O man, forswear thy foolish ways."

In fact, the song was written in 1916 by English poet Clifford Bax as a plaintive call to nations involved in World War I:

> Age after age their tragic empires rise,
> Built while they dream, and in that dreaming weep:
> Would man but wake from out his haunted sleep.

And those 1916 lyrics were derived from Ezekiel 33:11: "Turn! Turn from your evil ways!"

During this time of Easter, let's not think of conversion as just that salvation moment in our past history. Sure, Jesus's glorious work on the cross has saved us once for all. But let's humbly consider our current need for turning.

Let's consider our own foolish ways. Let's look at the idols we keep secret in our lives. We would do well to heed the call to confess our sins and turn back to God.

Preparing Your Heart for Easter

Lord God, I confess to you that I have been keeping idols in my life. I know I have given my life to you, and you have saved me. But I know as well that I continue to sin, and I need to turn form those foolish ways and convert my life, once again, toward your direction.

28
Sacrifice

Offer your bodies as a living sacrifice,
holy and pleasing to God—this is your
true and proper worship.

ROMANS 12:1

The game of baseball is quietly losing one of its best plays, the sacrifice bunt. With a runner on base, the batter chooses not to take a full swing at the ball but instead makes soft contact, pushing the ball onto the infield grass. The batter is almost certainly thrown out at first base, but the runner advances a base and is more likely to score if the next batter gets a hit.

The sacrifice is still allowable, but no one does it anymore. The stat crunchers have decreed that the play gives up too much. The out is worth more than the base.

The whole idea of sacrifice may also be losing traction in society at large. Give something up to help someone else? Well, let's crunch the stats and see if it really helps the greater good.

Sacrifice might be *the* major theme of the Bible. The law of Moses set up an elaborate sacrificial system, the prophets complained that sacrifices were being made with impure motives, then Jesus became God's perfect sacrifice, and His followers are called to be living sacrifices.

Even before Moses, many ancient cultures had traditions of slaying animals on altars to appease their deities. But Leviticus codified the process for Israel. There were burnt offerings, grain offerings, peace offerings, sin offerings, and trespass offerings. Some of these were prescribed for annual festivals, such as Passover. All of them involved bringing something of value to the altar—either at the tabernacle or later the Jerusalem temple.

In Isaiah's opening chapter, God complains about the hypocrisy of His people: "I have no pleasure in the blood of bulls and lambs and goats. . . . Stop bringing meaningless offerings! Your incense is detestable to me" (Isaiah 1:11, 13).

God wanted hearts and lives, not blood and guts. "Stop doing wrong. Learn to do right; seek justice. Defend the oppressed" (vv. 16–17). For rich landlords who cheated the poor all year and then expected to bribe God with a big sacrifice— well, that was just a lot of bull.

Sacrifice is a foundational theme of the Easter season. We sacrifice something we otherwise value and crave. Perhaps we are that sacrificial baseball hitter, giving up something to help another. And the whole of Lent points to Jesus's sacrifice for us on the cross.

The key to it all is this idea that God wants lives, not symbols. As God said through another prophet, "I desire mercy, not sacrifice, and acknowledgment of God rather than burnt offerings" (Hosea 6:6).

Jesus quoted that passage more than once in His dealings with the hypocritical religious leaders He encountered. And yet He became the sacrifice that every other sacrifice pointed to. "God presented Christ as a sacrifice of atonement, through the shedding of his blood—to be received by faith" (Romans 3:25). Elsewhere, Paul called Christ "our Passover lamb" (1 Corinthians 5:7).

The book of Hebrews makes the point that Old Testament sacrifices had to be repeated year by year, festival by festival, but "Christ was sacrificed once to take away the sins of many" (9:28).

The story of sacrifice doesn't end there. We who follow Jesus are called to be "a living sacrifice" (Romans 12:1). We give our lives to God in worship and loving support of others. "Through Jesus, therefore, let us continually offer to God a sacrifice of praise—the fruit of lips that openly profess his name. And do not forget to do good and to share with others, for with such sacrifices God is pleased" (Hebrews 13:15–16).

Preparing Your Heart for Easter

Ask yourself the question, How can I give up myself to help someone else get closer to success? Take some time to think of possibilities. Make a plan to do something sacrificial for another. What if we all lived like that each day?

29
Nail

He has taken [our sin] away, nailing it to the cross.

COLOSSIANS 2:14

You might know the old aphorism "For want of a nail." As that story goes, a missing nail caused a horseshoe to fall off, which kept the horse from going into battle, which kept the rider from delivering the decisive blow, so the battle was lost, and the war was lost. All because a nail wasn't doing its job.

We might use the same approach to the story of the crucifixion of Jesus.

But let's talk a bit about nails first.

These fasteners go back to the beginning of history. In the Bible's fourth chapter we read of Tubal-Cain, "who forged all kinds of tools out of bronze and iron" (Genesis 4:22). Archaeologists confirm that nails were among the tools of the Bronze Age.

In one of the many grisly stories in the book of Judges, a homemaker named Jael became an Israelite hero by offering an enemy general a place to sleep—and then pounding a nail into his head (4:21). Well, it's described as a tent peg, basically a large nail.

Solomon built the temple, adorning its most holy place with gold—including gold nails (2 Chronicles 3:9).

Biblical nails also pointedly have application for our own spiritual condition.

In the conclusion to Ecclesiastes, the author compares wisdom to two pointy objects. "The words of the wise are like goads, their collected sayings like firmly embedded nails" (12:11). Goads were pointed sticks, like long nails, that shepherds used to poke errant sheep—like us. "We all, like sheep, have gone astray, each of us has turned to our own way" (Isaiah 53:6).

And of course nails hold things fast. They keep chairs from being rickety and walls from falling over. Like nails, God's wisdom solidifies our lives, providing some surety when our lives get wobbly.

Jesus knew all about nails. He worked with His stepfather as a carpenter (Matthew 13:55; Mark 6:3). The Greek word could be used for a builder, stonemason, or craftsman, but nails would have been part of His tool kit. It is part of the poetry of the gospel that this builder, who put so many lives back together, was fastened to a slab of wood with nails—and that was how He crafted the salvation of the world.

And so, in this time of Easter when we anticipate the tragedy and triumph of the cross, the nails that pierced Jesus's hands and feet become a kind of horrific beauty. Nails and flesh are real things in a real world. The reality of the torture attests to the walking-on-earth reality of Jesus Christ.

The disciple Thomas needed proof, so Jesus showed him the nail prints (John 20:24–29). Once again, nails find their way into this story. This wasn't some hologram of the risen Jesus, not a mass hallucination. The doubter could touch the scars. The crucified Jesus was truly back from the dead, as the nails bore witness.

For want of a nail . . . the war was lost? No, the war against sin and death was decidedly won when the Carpenter was nailed to a cross for our sins and lived again.

Preparing Your Heart for Easter

*Father, thank you for sending your Son, in
real physical flesh and being, to save me from
spiritual death. Help me to follow Him each day,
mindful of the price He paid for me.*

30
Passion

*Did not the Messiah have to suffer these things
and then enter his glory?*

LUKE 24:26

In 2004, a movie moved, inspired, and deeply bothered viewers. *The Passion of the Christ* presented, in bloody detail, the scourging and crucifixion of Jesus. For some, it was much too gory. Others received it as a difficult but helpful reminder of the pain our Savior suffered.

The film was well named. The word *passion* means "suffering." Through the ages, it has especially been attached to the suffering of Jesus. Classical music lovers are familiar with Bach's *St. Matthew Passion* and many other works based on the gospel accounts of Jesus's suffering.

There's also a second meaning in "the passion of the Christ." In modern times, passion often refers to love—the emotion someone feels from a deep desire for someone else. In this sense, the passion of the dying Christ could be understood as His undying love for us.

The word *passion* comes into English from the Latin *passus*, a form of the verb *patior*, "to experience something." At some point it took on the meaning of enduring something negative.

We can also trace *passion* back to a Greek word, *pascho*, which has a noun form, *pathos*. The word *pascho* and its related forms appear about fifty times in the New Testament, and are usually translated "suffer."

Multiple times, Jesus prepared His disciples for His passion by saying He would have to "go to Jerusalem and suffer many things" (Matthew 16:21). After His resurrection, Jesus taught two clueless disciples on the road to Emmaus: "Did not the Messiah have to suffer these things and then enter his glory?" (Luke 24:26). This became an essential part of the apostle Paul's preaching: "Paul went into the synagogue, and . . . he reasoned with them from the Scriptures, explaining and proving that the Messiah had to suffer and rise from the dead" (Acts 17:2–3).

One of the most popular philosophies in the few centuries before and after Jesus was Stoicism. The Stoics talked a lot about *pathos*, about human suffering—how to think about it, how to deal with it, and how to avoid it. They had a strong moral code, and some even ditched the Greek pantheon in favor of one God over all—but they had a hard time imagining that this God could ever suffer.

The apostle Paul spoke powerfully into the Grecian world, even debating with Stoics in Athens (Acts 17:18). Just up the coast, in Philippi, lived a group of Christians who got a letter from the apostle about how Jesus refused to cling to His divinity but willingly poured himself out into human flesh, humbling himself in suffering and death, "even death on a cross" (Philippians 2:8).

This is the true meaning of the passion: Christ endured grotesque suffering in order to save people He is passionate about. "For Christ also suffered once for sins, the righteous for the unrighteous, to bring you to God" (1 Peter 3:18).

Preparing Your Heart for Easter

Give time today to ponder the meaning of Christ's passion. Consider how His passion for you was so great that He suffered passionately on the cross. Talk with Him and thank Him for His extraordinary love for you.

> The last week of Lent, beginning with Palm Sunday and continuing through Easter Sunday, is sometimes called Passion Week. Palm Sunday is often also referred to as Passion Sunday.

31

Cross

For the message of the cross is foolishness to those who are perishing, but to us who are being saved it is the power of God.

1 CORINTHIANS 1:18

After meeting in borrowed spaces for years, a new church was finally planning to construct its own building. Looking at the plans, one committee member asked, "So where's the cross going?"

The pastor replied, "Why should we have a cross?"

Yes, he was being a wise guy, but he was also being a wise leader. He wanted people to think about why they needed a cross in a church.

"Well, we're Christians," people said. "Christian churches have crosses."

"You do realize," the pastor added, "that the cross was a form of capital punishment. It would be like posting an image of an electric chair or a noose."

It took a while, but finally someone said, "We are who we are because of Jesus dying on the cross for us. We have eternal life because He died on the cross. We can't forget that."

Bingo. That was the answer the pastor wanted. And the church now has a cross prominently displayed in its sanctuary.

Crucifixion started with the Medes and Persians five centuries before Jesus. Alexander the Great used it. The Greek word for cross, *stauros*, literally means "stake." A body could be affixed to this post in various ways. The crossbeam was apparently a later development.

The Romans made it an art form. The Roman philosopher Seneca, adviser to the emperor Nero, wrote that the "worst torture of all" was crucifixion.[14]

The two main goals of crucifixion were pain and public display. The dying process was extended in various ways, including the addition of a small seat or pedestal that allowed victims to push themselves up and breathe a bit longer. (Our word *excruciating* comes from the Latin word for a cross.)

Crosses were often set up on high places or along roads, where people could see the victims dying. Humiliation was the goal here, but also deterrence. Often a placard was placed at the top of the vertical post, announcing the person's crime (see Matthew 27:37), suggesting to would-be offenders, "This could be you."

As horrific as the physical crucifixion of Jesus was, we need to keep in mind the spiritual horror of what He went through. We don't know precisely what His spiritual ordeal was, and theologians have different views on this, but we take note of

Peter's words: "'He himself bore our sins' in his body on the cross" (1 Peter 2:24).

Many people were crucified in that time, enduring the torture and humiliation, but only one, Jesus, also bore our sins. He somehow suffered the spiritual punishment of us all.

So the crucifixion was a cruel execution, but that was just the beginning of what Jesus went through on the cross. No wonder He prayed in Gethsemane: "Father, if you are willing, take this cup from me" (Luke 22:42).

Before we spring for that trendy gold chain bearing a gold cross, we would do well, like that church congregation, to consider what wearing a cross really means.

The cross represents Christ's gruesome death but also His unfathomable suffering for our sin. Further, Jesus himself forecast what the cross means for us, His followers: "Whoever wants to be my disciple must deny themselves and take up their cross and follow me" (Matthew 16:24).

The cross of history is a symbol of cruel violence. The cross of Christianity is a symbol of a life of hardship in being a Jesus follower.

The one thing a cross is not is sentimental.

Preparing Your Heart for Easter

All of Lent points to the cross. How does a deeper consideration of the meaning of Christ's death on the cross affect your walk with Him today?

Lord Jesus, I'm thinking a bit differently about the cross now. It has more significance than I had considered. Help me to see your sacrifice on the cross in connection to my own challenges, the crosses in life I need to bear.

An old tradition says that Peter was executed in Rome around AD 66 by crucifixion—but he considered himself unworthy to die as Jesus did, so he asked to be crucified upside down.

32
Resurrection

You are looking for Jesus, who was crucified.
He is not here; he has risen.

MATTHEW 28:5-6

The story of God and us leads to an impossible climax. The Messiah was supposed to be this drama's triumphant ending. Now He is dead. Jesus was crucified and His body is held in a tomb.

A final act would require the unimaginable.

Every so often the Old Testament opens up a conversation with the New Testament.

Ezekiel saw dry bones come to life (37:10). In Daniel we read, "Multitudes who sleep in the dust of the earth will awake" (12:2). In a psalm quoted by early Christians, we find the prophecy, "You will not abandon me to the realm of the dead, nor will you let your faithful one see decay" (16:10). Beset by misfortunes, Job argued his innocence before skeptical friends. Then he said something surprising: "I know that my redeemer lives, and that in the end he will stand on the earth" (19:25). And in another stunning Old-to-New-Testament time warp, Hosea said, "After two days [the Lord] will revive us; on the third day he will restore us, that we may live in his presence" (6:2).

It's the Old telling the New what might, just might, be possible.

In the New Testament, before Holy Week, there were hints of what was to come. Jesus raised several people to life: The daughter of a synagogue official. The son of a widow. Some skeptics suggest that He was just reviving people who seemed dead. Maybe they were saying the same thing back then, because Jesus waited a few days—until decay set in—before raising Lazarus.[15]

Of course, when the New Testament mentions resurrection, it's usually talking about Jesus coming back to life after His crucifixion. Two different words are used. When the emphasis is on God "raising up" Jesus, we find forms of the Greek word *egeiro*. But sometimes it refers to Jesus "rising" from the dead. This is the compound verb *anistemi* or, in its noun form, *anastasia*. Both of these words literally mean "to stand again."

Again, the Old Testament and New Testament are in conversation. Do you hear echoes of Job? The Redeemer would literally "stand on the earth" again, even after dying for our sins.

We awaken on Sunday morning, and it turns out this true-life drama *does* have a final act.

"After the Sabbath, at dawn on the first day of the week, Mary Magdalene and the other Mary went to look at the tomb" (Matthew 28:1). There was a violent earthquake, the tombstone was rolled away, and an angel appeared "like lightning" (v. 3).

The guards at the tomb were so afraid they were shaking, and we're told, perhaps with a touch of irony, they "became like dead men" (v. 4).

The angel told the women, "Do not be afraid. . . . He has risen" (vv. 5–6).

The unimaginable just happened. The impossible was made possible. Death became life. And in our lives today, Jesus appears and greets us, offering us life—eternal life.

Preparing Your Heart for Easter

For you today, the resurrection isn't just an assurance of heaven after you die. It's a promise of power for your earthly life right now. Paul writes, "And if the Spirit of him who raised Jesus from the dead is living in you, he who raised Christ from the dead will also give life to your mortal bodies because of his Spirit who lives in you" (Romans 8:11).

Lord God, how can I live out the truth of
the resurrection today?

33
Palm

They took palm branches and went out to meet him, shouting, "Hosanna!" "Blessed is he who comes in the name of the Lord!"

JOHN 12:13

Our early memories of Palm Sunday, perhaps yours as well, are of a sanctuary decorated with greenery, and somehow (despite that we lived in the Northeast United States) tropical branches of actual palm trees adorned the altar in front.

Palm Sunday was a happy day, a hosanna day, a respite after a long, hard Lenten period of introspection, confession, and mourning.

It is that indeed, but it's also a brief jolt of joy before the storm.

The palm branches of that first Palm Sunday would have come from the date palm, which is common in the region around Jerusalem. The tree has a sturdy trunk that rises sixty to ninety feet and then sprouts with leafy fronds that can grow upward another six feet. It produces large clusters of dates, and a fibrous part of the tree can be woven into a strong rope.

The tree was so common in the Middle East that it was often illustrated in carvings and coinage, going back millennia (see 1 Kings 6:29). Columns of ancient buildings were often made to look like palm trees, topped by capitals resembling the leafy fronds.

It's those branches that play a role in the Jesus account, as He rode into the city on a donkey. "They took palm branches and went out to meet him, shouting, 'Hosanna!' 'Blessed is he who comes in the name of the Lord!' 'Blessed is the king of Israel!'" (John 12:13).[16]

These were the Jesus followers, some of the multitudes who had traipsed with Him across the region, drinking in the wine of His words and eating up the bread of His promise of a new life. These were Jews and Gentiles who believed Him to be the long-awaited Messiah. They were giving Him the red-carpet treatment.

The practice of laying palms had a history among the Jewish people.

Back in the books of Moses, instructions were given for a weeklong harvest festival. "On the first day you are to take branches from luxuriant trees—from palms, willows and other leafy trees—and rejoice before the LORD your God for seven days" (Leviticus 23:40). (They were also instructed to use the branches to create temporary structures, and this became known as the Feast of Booths. It's also sometimes called the Feast of Tabernacles.)

So the Jews were used to celebrating God's blessings by waving branches and singing praises while joining in a grand procession.

To the Jesus followers of that first Palm Sunday, this celebration marked the arrival of a redeeming king. In the prophetic words of Zechariah, "See, your king comes to you, righteous and victorious, lowly and riding on a donkey. . . . He will proclaim peace to the nations" (9:9–10).

But you may hear a few minor chords in the soundtrack to this movie. For all the throngs lining the path with palms, there were other factions of Jews and Romans who had a different idea about Jesus—a different plan for Him in the week ahead.

Further, for these adoring worshippers, Jesus was not the kind of king they were expecting. They envisioned the Messiah as a political leader, the head of state. This walk into Jerusalem, they believed, was the beginning of a new government.

But Jesus would soon appear to these worshippers as far less than their king—even though He is so much more. Indeed, Jesus defies all our expectations. The irony of the ages is that this conqueror won peace not with a sword but with a cross, not by killing His enemies but by forgiving them, not by avoiding death but by giving His life for humankind . . . for us.

Preparing Your Heart for Easter

Lord God, help me ponder during this Palm Sunday how Jesus defies my own expectations, how He challenges my assumptions, and how He might transform my life in new ways.

34

Hosanna

*The crowds that went ahead of him
and those that followed shouted,
"Hosanna to the Son of David!"*

MATTHEW 21:9

That first Palm Sunday, "a very large crowd spread their cloaks on the road, while others cut branches from the trees and spread them on the road. The crowds that went ahead of him and those that followed shouted, 'Hosanna to the Son of David!' 'Blessed is he who comes in the name of the Lord!' 'Hosanna in the highest heaven!'" (Matthew 21:8–9).

This celebration resembles the Feast of Tabernacles (or Booths), observed each autumn. It was a harvest festival, and people would grab branches to wave in the opening procession, and then use these branches to build temporary shelters for the rest of the week.

What we call the triumphal entry happened in the spring, shortly before Passover, so maybe this was sort of a flash mob that gathered to welcome Jesus, using the practices they were familiar with from their harvest parade.

But what is this strange word they were shouting? *Hosanna*?

It derives from a Hebrew phrase that comes right out of Psalm 118—*hoshiya na*—which literally means "Help now!" or "Save us please!" (see v. 25).

The Hebrew term *hoshiya* was commonly used as a request for deliverance. In Psalm 12 the writer uses it in what seems to be a pretty bad time: "Help, LORD, for no one is faithful anymore; those who are loyal have vanished from the human race" (v. 1). When Isaiah says, "Surely the arm of the LORD is not too short to save" (59:1), he's using that word. Elsewhere, a woman gains an audience with King David and begins with "Help me, Your Majesty!" (2 Samuel 14:4), using the same word.

But the way it's used in the Palm Sunday account, *hosanna* seems like a shout of praise, not a cry for help. It's offered *to* the Son of David. It rings through "the highest heaven." It sounds like they're saying, "Praise you!" or (to use another Hebrew term) "Hallelujah!"

This makes sense when you think about it. When you need help, where do you turn? To someone bigger, smarter, stronger—someone who is able to rescue you from your difficulty.

John Piper notes this shift in the meaning of the word: "Something happened to that phrase, *hoshiya na*. The meaning changed over the years. In [Psalm 118] it was immediately followed by the exclamation: 'Blessed is he who comes in the name of the Lord!' The cry for help, *hoshiya na*, was answered almost before it came out of the psalmist's mouth. And over the centuries the phrase *hoshiya na* stopped being a cry for help in the ordinary language of the Jews. Instead it became a shout of hope and exultation."[17]

Imagine a different kind of procession. You're living in a French town in 1945. Your country has been occupied by the Nazis for several years, but the Allies have finally broken through to liberate your town. As the Allied troops roll through, the people line the streets, shouting, "Save us! We love you! Thank you! You are victorious! Hooray!"

That's what *hosanna* means.

See, it's more than a word study. This mash-up of Hebrew and Greek words expresses the reality we find ourselves in.

The original Hebrew meaning expresses our desperate heart need. Some scholars say *hoshiya na* also carries a sense of urgency: "I am broken and desperate. Please save me *now*."

The Greek meaning of *hosanna* expresses the relief that our help has come. Jesus has rescued us from our brokenness. He promises new life, a new direction. Hosanna is our outburst of excitement, a giddy exuberance in the amazing news that Jesus Christ is here to save.

Preparing Your Heart for Easter

Perhaps you feel that desperate, urgent need for help today. Your heart is broken, your life is broken, and you cry out. Perhaps your use of the word *hosanna* now takes on new depth. Bring this into your prayer time with God. Cry out to Him in your brokenness and need for help. Cry out to Him in your joy that He has come to save you. Say it aloud—in fact, shout it!—and make it your exuberant exclamation to the one who has saved you.

35
New

The old has gone, the new is here!

2 CORINTHIANS 5:17

Does the world of advertising have any better word than *new*? We want the latest, greatest products in their new, improved versions. The technology explosion of the last few decades has made newness even more important. People are embarrassed to be seen with a flip phone, a bulky TV, or a CD player when there are newer gadgets available.

New is also a key word in the Bible. While Scripture shows respect for God-given traditions, it also reveals that the Creator is still creative, constantly doing new things for us, around us, and within us. Jesus once said that a Bible student who truly follows Him is like a homeowner rooting through an attic and pulling out "new treasures as well as old" (Matthew 13:52).

You might think of the Old Testament as, you know, *old*, but God's penchant for newness flows through it, especially in the Prophets. "See, I am doing a new thing!" God announces through Isaiah (43:19). He was promising to lead His people out of their captivity in Babylon and renew their ruined homeland.

Wandering through those ruins, Jeremiah wept, but he also summoned hope in the wake of disaster. "Because of the LORD's great love we are not consumed, for his compassions never fail. They are new every morning; great is your faithfulness" (Lamentations 3:22–23). God still showed His love in new ways.

God wasn't just rebuilding Jerusalem. His big-picture plan, echoed in New Testament prophecy, is to "create new heavens and a new earth," where the "former things"—like destruction and punishment—"will not be remembered, nor will they come to mind" (Isaiah 65:17).

New Testament writers had two words for "new" available to them. *Neos* refers to recency, something younger, this year's model. But *kainos* is the word they chose almost all the time. This means "new and different," a new kind of thing. You can see how the life-changing, world-changing work of Jesus had to be described with this level of *kainos* newness.

Jesus gave new meaning to the Passover tradition when he raised a cup of wine and spoke of "the new covenant in my blood" (Luke 22:20).

He gave His disciples a "new command" to love one another (John 13:34).

And Peter praised God for giving us a "new birth into a living hope through the resurrection of Jesus Christ from the dead" (1 Peter 1:3).

One of the last word pictures we see in Scripture is God

on His throne, overseeing "a new heaven and a new earth" (Revelation 21:1). He says, "I am making everything new!" (v. 5).

This echoes the words of Isaiah earlier—"I am doing a new thing!"—knitting together the plan and purpose of the entire Bible.

Preparing Your Heart for Easter

Perhaps you consider yourself a Christ follower and have given your heart to Jesus. But maybe you have strayed away and fallen into some old things. This culmination of the Easter season is the perfect time for you to respond to God and allow Him to change you, to reclaim you anew. In your recommitment to Him, you will be able to sing once more, "Morning by morning new mercies I see."

Lord God, help me be open to new things you have for me in my life.

The poetry of Lamentations 3:23 echoes in the hymn "Great Is Thy Faithfulness": "Morning by morning new mercies I see."

Thomas Chisholm, a humble teacher and pastor from Kentucky, wrote the lyrics to that great hymn. He sent this poem to William Runyan, a musician with ties to Chicago's Moody Bible

Institute, and Runyan liked the work and put it to music.

Later, Runyan's connection to Billy Graham led to the hymn being used at Graham rallies, and "Great Is Thy Faithfulness" became a popular favorite.

36
Salvation

How much more, having been reconciled,
shall we be saved through his life!

ROMANS 5:10

In Major League Baseball, a team will often bring in one of their best pitchers at the end of a close game. If this hurler succeeds in shutting down the opponents' bats and securing the victory, he is credited with a save.

Over a brilliant nineteen-year career with the New York Yankees, Mariano Rivera was the best at this, amassing 652 saves—and prompting signs to pop up in the stands that said, "Only Jesus saves more than Mariano."

Rivera, a man of deep faith, was probably embarrassed by that statement, but he'd surely agree that Jesus is the all-time "saves" leader.

Hebrew has a family of words for "save," "savior," and "salvation" (*yasha*, *moshiya*, *yeshua*). These words are related to other terms for health and well-being. So God is hailed as the Savior who looks out for the welfare of His chosen people in various ways.

Safe on the far shore of the Red Sea after a miraculous

escape from Egypt, the Israelites sang, "The LORD is my strength and my defense; he has become my salvation [*yeshua*]" (Exodus 15:2). Throughout the Old Testament, salvation refers to help in times of trouble. At a national level, God saves His people Israel from foreign armies—like that Egyptian battalion swept away by the sea.

In New Testament Greek we find a similar word family (*sozo, soter, soteria*), but the meaning is significantly different.

"Today salvation has come to this house," Jesus said at the home of Zacchaeus, a tax collector who had just repented of his fraudulent ways (Luke 19:9). Clearly this was a personal conversion, not a defeat of enemy armies. Jesus went on to recite His own mission statement: "For the Son of Man came to seek and to save the lost" (v. 10).

The saving is not just a cure for a plague or a bumper crop to end a famine. It's more than physical welfare. It's spiritual. Lives are changed. When people are lost, like Zacchaeus, the Savior finds them and reconnects them with God. After an encounter with Jesus, a group of Samaritans said, "We know that this man really is the Savior of the world" (John 4:42).

Not just Israel. The world.

The whole story of Jesus is wrapped up in this language of salvation.

"Today in the town of David a Savior has been born to

you," an angel announced to a band of stunned shepherds (Luke 2:11). An old prophet at the temple took the baby Jesus in his arms and prayed, "My eyes have seen your salvation, which you have prepared in the sight of all nations, a light for revelation to the Gentiles, and the glory of your people Israel" (vv. 30–32). Even then, the promise of salvation extended beyond the one nation of Israel.

In the months and years after Jesus's death and resurrection, the apostles made it clear that these events brought salvation to the world. "Salvation is found in no one else," Peter preached, "for there is no other name under heaven given to mankind by which we must be saved" (Acts 4:12).

Paul and Barnabas described how God had commissioned their ministry: "I have made you a light for the Gentiles, that you may bring salvation to the ends of the earth" (Acts 13:47).

On this journey to Easter, we are reminded of our spiritual need and how we, on our own, are lost. We need saving. But we come to understand the death and resurrection of Jesus not only as momentous, miraculous events but also as *saving* events, the extraordinary rescue mission God has engineered to save us, whom He loves.

Preparing Your Heart for Easter

Lord God, in this season of remembering the death and resurrection of your Son, help me deeply embrace the full meaning of salvation.

37
Maundy

A new command I give you: Love one another.
JOHN 13:34

Every Holy Week, as Christians observe the momentous events of the death and resurrection of Jesus, one soul-stirring question afflicts the hearts and minds of millions: What does *maundy* mean?

Since the Middle Ages, the day before Good Friday has been known as Maundy Thursday. Many have assumed that *maundy* is just an old-timey word for "holy." Not so. Others, noting the somber tones of Maundy Thursday services—for instance, the stripping of the altar in many churches—figure that *maundy* must mean "sorrowful." Nope.

The word comes from the Latin for something Jesus said on the first Maundy Thursday. In the Vulgate, the Bible translation used in Western medieval churches, John 13:34 begins, "Mandatum novum do vobis." Or, as a modern translation puts it: "A new command I give you." *Mandatum*, or its verb form *mandare*, "to command," became *maundy*.

The Jewish faith was anchored by the law of God, commandments given to Moses and shared with God's people. In

Jesus's day, the Pharisees saw themselves as guardians of those commandments, and they added a few of their own just to be on the safe side. Though Jesus assured His hearers that He had not come "to abolish the Law or the Prophets . . . but to fulfill them" (Matthew 5:17), He often criticized the Pharisees for missing the point of God's Word. In their zeal to keep the rules, they neglected the relationship God wanted with them.

So it was no small matter that, on the eve of the day that would pave the way to eternal life, Jesus issued a new *mandatum*. With His death as the sacrificial Lamb of God, He was about to fulfill the requirements of the law of Moses and take away the sin of the world (John 1:29). But there was a new command for those who trusted Him: *love one another*.

This is what makes Thursday "maundy."

"As I have loved you, so you must love one another," Jesus added. "By this everyone will know that you are my disciples, if you love one another" (John 13:34–35).

This is the new command, summarizing and fulfilling the old commands. Our life choices are now compelled by our love for God rather than the fear of displeasing Him—because "perfect love drives out fear" (1 John 4:18).

Maundy Thursday is also associated with the Last Supper, specifically the act of foot washing that Jesus performed with His disciples: "He poured water into a basin and began to wash his disciples' feet, drying them with the towel that was wrapped around him" (John 13:5).

On Maundy Thursday, some churches reenact the Lord's Supper, including the rite of foot washing. It is a humble acknowledgment of the new commandment.

Indeed, the "maundiness" of Thursday is not in its holiness or sadness, but in the love of the sacrifice Jesus willingly made for us. And in His charge to us to show the same love to others.

Elesha Coffman writes, "It's common to hear from the pulpit that no one can fully appreciate the joy of Easter Sunday without experiencing the darkness of Good Friday. But the disciples would have been bewildered by both without the lesson of Holy Thursday. The day they received the command to love, had their feet washed by a king, and first understood the link between the Passover sacrifice, Christ, and the bread of life, shouldn't be missed by any of us, even if the calendar shows a blank square."[18]

Preparing Your Heart for Easter

Take a moment to consider the people closest to you. What would it mean for you actually to kneel before them with a pail of water and, with the commandment on your lips to "love one another," wash their feet?

Lord, direct me to someone today to whom
I might show the love you speak of, the love
that echoes my love for you.

38
Good

At noon, darkness fell across the whole land
until three o'clock. . . . Then Jesus shouted out
again, and he released his spirit.

MATTHEW 27:45, 50 NLT

Since Good Friday is all about the horrible suffering Jesus went through, why do we call it "good"?

Perhaps you've heard the question. Perhaps you've asked it yourself. There's no definitive answer, but experts have come up with some working theories.

The earliest use of the term that we know about ("guode Friday") occurred in the *South English Legendary* in about AD 1290, according to the *Oxford English Dictionary*, which keeps track of these things. The day was "good" because the church recognized it as a holy day. Holy is good. Others suggest the day was first called "God's Friday," which eventually elided into "good."

Whatever the origin of the name, many Christians have no problem with it. While we are saddened each year by the cruelty inflicted on our beloved Lord Jesus, we also recognize that this was the day He saved us. Our eternal life was won on Good Friday. The powers of evil did their worst, but they could not vanquish God's goodness. "'He himself bore our sins' in his body on the cross, so that we might die to sins and

live for righteousness; 'by his wounds you have been healed'"
(1 Peter 2:24).

When the Bible describes creation in its first chapter,
there's a repeated theme. After each day of God's work, "God
saw that it was good." The Hebrew word for "good," *tov*, is
nothing fancy. It's just saying that, day by day, the growing
universe was pleasant, positive, lovely, in working order. After
the sixth day, however, the formula changes slightly: "God saw
all that he had made, and it was very good" (Genesis 1:31).
Perhaps this refers to the totality of creation—it was God's last
day before resting—but remember that human beings were
created on that last day. The world, now with humanity in it,
was an extra level of good.

And it's probably no accident that, in the Bible's second
chapter, the Lord says, "It is not good for the man to be alone.
I will make a helper suitable for him" (Genesis 2:18). People
are made for community, fellowship, friendship, love. As the
psalmist says, "How good [*tov*] and pleasant it is when God's
people live together in unity!" (Psalm 133:1).

An affluent young man ran up to Jesus and asked, "Good
teacher, . . . what must I do to inherit eternal life?" (Mark
10:17).

There are a few Greek words translated "good." *Kalos* is
one, often paired with *kakos* ("bad"). You might translate it as

"pretty," "not bad," or "good enough." But that's not the word used in this story.

This word—*agathos*—is far more complimentary. You might say "excellent," "outstanding," "praiseworthy." The young man calls Jesus an excellent, outstanding teacher and asks a basic Sabbath-school question. Jesus offers an odd response: "Why do you call me good? . . . No one is good— except God alone" (v. 18).

Perhaps Jesus was cutting through the fluffy compliment to get to the heart of the matter. Was this young man just surveying the local rabbis to get a good deal on the hereafter? Or was he truly willing to do what an excellent God required? Perhaps there's a touch of irony in Jesus's response: "Only God is good, and you're calling me good. Do you really know who you're talking to?

As it turns out, the young man didn't.

Good Friday was a terrible, horrible, no good, very bad day—and the best thing that ever happened to humankind. Only in the death of Jesus Christ could death be conquered for us all. Only after the terrible events of that Friday could that Sunday be a new dawning for the world.

Easter Sunday makes Friday so very good.

There's another Bible verse quoted so often that many of us forget how awesome it is. "And we know that God causes all things to work together for good [*agathos*] to those who love God, to those who are called according to His purpose" (Romans 8:28 NASB).

Bad things happen in our lives. The Bible never denies that. And this verse is not telling us that the *kalos* will outweigh the *kakos*, so our lives will be "pretty" or "good enough." No, it's reminding us that God has a level of goodness far beyond what we know. He is crafting that level of eternal excellence, and we're a part of it.

Nothing can separate us from His loving purpose. Not even a crucifixion.

And that's why Good Friday is good.

Preparing Your Heart for Easter

Lord, I come to you today deeply aware of the wounds you suffered on the cross—not only the piercings of your flesh but the terrible pain of taking on my sin and the sins of the world. Thank you for your redeeming goodness . . . Here, today, are my wounds, my hurts, my agonies.

39
Tomb

They found the stone rolled away from the tomb, but when they entered, they did not find the body of the Lord Jesus.

LUKE 24:2-3

The universally recognized symbol of Christianity is the cross, and with good reason. But if we ever need a second symbol, perhaps we could nominate the empty tomb. It doesn't fit so well on a neck chain, and it looks weird on a T-shirt, but it stands for another key element in our faith. Jesus didn't just die for our sins. He rose from the dead to give us new life.

The Greek word for tomb is *mnemeion*, related to the word *memory*. That fits. A tomb serves as a memorial for a deceased loved one. We all know bodies decay after death. What remains is the memory of a person. Often a grave marker, a headstone, or even a mausoleum can preserve that memory.

Ironically, the most memorable thing about Jesus's tomb is its emptiness. It was a temporary resting place, a three-day stay.

In biblical times, some bodies were buried in the ground, with the place marked by a tree or pile of stones. Parts of Israel had rocky, mountainous terrain with caves and caverns. These made good tombs.

Israel's law cautioned against touching dead bodies. This made a person "unclean" and required a substantial cleansing process. So it was important to warn people when they were near a tomb. Some cave tombs were whitewashed each spring for this purpose. Jesus once said to the hypocritical Pharisees, "You are like whitewashed tombs, which look beautiful on the outside but on the inside are full of the bones of the dead and everything unclean" (Matthew 23:27).

People of wealth could afford to pay a stonemason to cut a tomb into a rocky outcropping. (Much of the rock in Israel is limestone, so this wouldn't have been as labor-intensive as it seems.) Joseph of Arimathea, a secret follower of Jesus, is described as "a rich man" and "a prominent member" of the Jewish Council, with "his own new tomb that he had cut out of the rock" (Matthew 27:57, 60; Mark 15:43). He arranged with the Roman governor to take Jesus's body from the cross and place it there.

With cave tombs—either natural or cut into a hillside—it was common to attach some sort of door. This might be of wood or stone, square or circular. The door discouraged grave robbers and anyone who might wander in by accident and become contaminated. In the case of Jesus's tomb, much is made of the fact that a large stone was rolled in front of the tomb and sealed in place. But the visitors on Sunday morning found it "rolled away" (Mark 16:4).

Think about three words, all places where Jesus spent time: womb, room, and tomb:

1. The Son of God went through the very human process of gestation in Mary's *womb*.

2. He was laid in a feed bin because "there was no guest *room* available for them" (Luke 2:7, emphasis added). Years later, in the upper room, He gave new meaning to the Passover meal.

3. Then the *tomb*, where He won the ultimate victory over death.

The story of Jesus in three rhyming words.

Preparing Your Heart for Easter

Have you kept Jesus Christ buried somewhere in your life? Is He a dormant part of your past faith, now hidden from public view? What would it take for you to roll away the tombstone and proclaim Jesus Christ openly as your resurrected Lord?

On a website for the construction of mausoleums, a company lists ten reasons to consider them for the project. These include quality of materials, thicker walls, and expert craftwork. Number ten is an "eternal guarantee," noting that the mausoleums they build are protected "in perpetuity."

Followers of Christ know better and see the irony: our eternal guarantee is based on Jesus Christ making His tomb temporary.

40

Easter

The Word became flesh and made his dwelling among us. We have seen his glory, the glory of the one and only Son, who came from the Father, full of grace and truth.

JOHN 1:14

Funny what happens to holidays. They accrue all sorts of traditions that sometimes obscure the original meaning.

No doubt this holiday you'll see someone dressed up as the Easter Bunny. Some hunt for Easter eggs or pig out on Easter candy. For sale are Easter lilies and Easter hams. Some make a tradition of streaming the old movie *Easter Parade* (Fred Astaire and Judy Garland putting on a show).

Culture has a way of taking profound spiritual reality and converting it into trivial pursuit. That isn't the true Easter, we protest.

But do we really know what Easter is about?

Every spring, in its northern latitudes, the earth puts on a pageant. Death and rebirth are enacted in bud and blade. Plants that seemed to die in a harsh winter suddenly sprout to life again. The sun rises in the east, bringing warmth and energy to a worn world.

It seems that the Saxons of Northern Europe and the British Isles honored a goddess of the east, calling her Eostre. We can imagine them holding a festival for her each spring, tossing off their heavy coats for more colorful garb, decorating everything with the flowers and greenery of the new season.

In the sixth century, Pope Gregory sent monks to England for the purpose of converting the local tribes to Christianity. It was then that the spring celebrations of the north became the Christian celebration of the resurrected Christ.

While we don't believe in the goddess Eostre, we do believe in God's creation of the world and of seasons. There's something wonderful and meaningful about how nature itself is hardwired to celebrate resurrection every year. "For since the creation of the world God's invisible qualities—his eternal power and divine nature—have been clearly seen, being understood from what has been made" (Romans 1:20).

In the events leading to His crucifixion, Jesus celebrated the Jewish Passover with His friends. Then He went out to pray, was arrested, crucified, and laid in a tomb. But on Sunday morning the tomb was empty. Jesus had risen. He had conquered death, and now He invited everyone into a new, eternal life.

Since most of the early Christians were Jewish, they connected the celebration of Jesus's resurrection with their annual Passover meal, reading a new, Christ-centered meaning into the old rituals. Eventually it became a separate celebration, though still scheduled near Passover time.

The seasonal holiday of Easter became one and the same with the Christian Passover celebration of Jesus's resurrection.

Whatever the origins and history of Easter, what matters is the extraordinary meaning of the reality of the resurrection: Jesus's death on the cross was an act of God to restore what we have defiled, to right the mess we've made of everything, and to reunite us with our loving God.

Yet none of that means squat unless Jesus Christ himself conquered death. If He is just a corpse in a tomb, He is not God. And this is the suspense of Easter week: the long silence of Saturday after the death of Jesus on Friday, like a slow ticking of a clock . . .

Easter Sunday dawns. We stand at the tomb alongside Jesus's mother, Mary Magdalene, and the other women. The tomb is open. Empty. We hear the words, "He is risen!"

This, then, is the true meaning of Easter. Christ has conquered death. God has provided a way for us to be with Him eternally. Christ is risen!

He is risen indeed.

Preparing Your Heart for Easter

Lord God, there are no words within me that are sufficient to express my joy and gratefulness. Christ is alive—risen from the dead and alive in my heart! Thank you.

Notes

1. Eugene Peterson, *Tell It Slant: A Conversation on the Language of Jesus in His Stories and Prayers* (Grand Rapids, MI: Eerdmans, 2012), 238.

2. Thomas McKenzie, *Lent with the Desert Fathers* (Nashville: Colony Catherine, 2019), 98.

3. N. T. Wright, *Lent for Everyone: Mark, Year B* (Louisville, KY: Westminster John Knox Press, 2012), 15.

4. Some translations use "declare" instead of "confess," but it's the same word translated "confess" elsewhere—*homologeo*, "to say the same thing."

5. Martin Luther, "Sermon on the Sacrament of Penance," in *The Roots of Reform*, edited by Timothy J. Wengert (Minneapolis, MN: Fortress Press, 2015), 189.

6. Oswald Chambers, *My Utmost for His Highest*, edited by James Reimann (Grand Rapids, MI: Discovery House, 1992), 155.

7. McKenzie, *Lent with the Desert Fathers*, 80.

8. Tim Keller, "Holiness; Overview," Gospel in Life, May 20, 2020, https://podcast.gospelinlife.com/e/holiness-overview/.

9. Kathleen Norris, "Holy Week and Easter," in *God for Us: Rediscovering the Meaning of Lent and Easter*, ed. Greg Pennoyer and Gregory Wolfe (Orleans, MA: Paraclete Press, 2015), 196–97.

10. Keith Potter, "Holy God," *Devotions for Lent from Holy Bible: Mosaic*, YouVersion, accessed May 27, 2022, https://www.bible.com/reading-plans/105-devotions-for-lent-from-holy-bible-mosaic/day/22.

11. Ronald Rolheiser, introduction to *God for Us*, 4.

12. Len Woods, *101 Important Words of the Bible: And the Unforgettable Story They Tell* (Grand Rapids, MI: Our Daily Bread Publishing, 2020), 25.

13. Scott Cairns, "Third Week of Lent," in *God with Us*, 87.

14. Stephen M. Miller, *Eyewitness to Crucifixion: The Romans, the Cross, and the Sacrifice of Jesus* (Grand Rapids, MI: Our Daily Bread Publishing, 2020), 1.

15. In one of the odd ironies of the Gospels, after the raising of Lazarus, the religious leaders plotted to kill him—to make him dead again—to neutralize this living testimony of the power of Jesus.

16. All four gospels tell about this triumphal entry, but only John specifically mentions palm branches. Matthew and Mark just say "branches," and Luke only talks about the cloaks spread on the ground in front of Jesus (Matthew 21:7; Mark 11:8; Luke 19:36). Perhaps this is because Luke was a Gentile aware of his Gentile readership; Jewish readers would have understood the palm branches in a way that others wouldn't have.

17. John Piper, "Hosanna! Palm Sunday," Desiring God, March 27, 1983, https://www.desiringgod.org/messages/hosanna.

18. Elesha Coffman, "The Other Holy Day," *Christianity Today*, March 1, 2002, https://www.christianitytoday.com/ct/2002/marchweb-only/3-18-52.0.html.

Permissions

Help us get the word out!

Our Daily Bread Publishing exists to feed the soul with the Word of God.

If you appreciated this book, please let others know.

- Pick up another copy to give as a gift.
- Share a link to the book or mention it on social media.
- Write a review on your blog, on a book-seller's website, or at our own site (odb.org/store).
- Recommend this book for your church, book club, or small group.

Connect with us:

f @ourdailybread

⊙ @ourdailybread

𝕏 @ourdailybread

Our Daily Bread Publishing
PO Box 3566
Grand Rapids, Michigan 49501 USA

✉ books@odb.org